THE PICK OF PUNCH

THE PICK OF
PUNCH

AN ANNUAL SELECTION
EDITED BY
NICOLAS BENTLEY

ANDRE DEUTSCH

FIRST PUBLISHED 1959 BY ANDRE DEUTSCH LIMITED
12–14 CARLISLE STREET SOHO SQUARE LONDON W1

© BRADBURY, AGNEW & COMPANY LTD 1959

PRINTED IN GREAT BRITAIN BY
BRADBURY AGNEW PRESS LIMITED LONDON

Introduction

THE MOST generally disliked man I ever met was a member of a little English community we had due south-west of Potsdam in the old days—ten years at least before our fellow Nordics suddenly handed their *Gemuetlichkeit* to the cloakroom attendant and commenced firing at us from the hip.

It was a time when a man having talent and a burned match to smudge his lip with could keep the table in a roar by just pulling a lock of hair down over his forehead, shooting his arm out horizontally, and saying '*Heil ich!*' I mean it made people laugh.

What chiefly kept us together as a group of British men and women whose business had brought us to live in Germany, were a number of charitable enterprises we had—bridge tournaments and raffles, with proceeds going to down-and-out British exiles. About these we had an unstinted feeling. When the beneficiary is certified as down, and genuinely out for the count, you take your raffle ticket without a nagging fear lest he make a comeback and grab your job as agent in Germany for Brown's Universal Powders.

We also had the Frothblowers' Club. Unless you are already of mature years and fairly well-travelled, you are going to find a little difficulty in believing that what I say about the importance of the Frothblowers in British life abroad at that period is factual. And I can see why.

One presumed, rightly or wrongly, that the Frothblowers had been originated by the brewers. Wherever the idea may have originated, it had soon taken off and was playing a rôle right round the world. It catered—and the behaviour of this much-disliked man Chones was proof of it—for people's desire to join something; join anything. It was the apotheosis of Togetherness. Its functions and objectives were as abstract as a Platonic Idea. It did not, strictly speaking, make sense.

There was a ritual, naturally, connected with beer-drinking, and for special occasions you could buy Frothblowers' cuff-links for your evening shirt. It also had an anthem, of which the words were, in the most restricted sense of the word, memorable; the phrase, 'the more we are together' was repeated three times, followed by the statement 'the merrier we shall be.' For membership, so far as British nationals were concerned, there were, to my know-ledge no qualifications at all. Yet Chones was excluded.

There were many Englishmen abroad who did not want to be Frothblowers. Chones was the only one in, I believe, the whole world who wanted to be a Frothblower but could not. For him forms and formalities were invented which nobody else bothered about. And once when he actually appeared at the hotel where the Frothblowers' annual dinner was being held, he, and he alone, was asked for his membership card, and turned out.

He sat all evening in a café across the street and listened to the Frothblowers' German guests—there were always dozens of them, speaking of their love for England and telling people not to worry about Hitler—singing, 'Ze more we are zoo*getter*, zoo*getter*, zoo*getter*. . .'

There was no apparent reason for the Froth-blowers' hatred of Chones other than the fact that, as one got to know both them and him a little better, he began to seem rather less of a clod, less, if one may say so, entirely benthic than they were. For his part, in a love-hate relationship such as the psycho-analysts were then telling us all about, he simul-taneously longed to join the Frothblowers, and viewed them with hatred and contempt. And he planned revenge.

'Take a look at that' he said to me one day, handing me some forty pages of foolscap corroded with vitriol. Keeping a fair balance between the criminally libellous and the merely obscene, the opus delineated the Frothblowers—organisationally and individually.

'I'm sending it,' said Chones, 'to *Punch*.'

'You think . . . ?' I said diffidently.

'Right up their street,' said Chones.

When the offering was returned we were both unsurprised, but for different reasons.

'See that?' Chones said. 'The Editor *regrets*. Get the significance? Wanted to publish it. Saw it was right up their street. But there you are. Outside pressure. City interests. Downing Street. What d'you expect when an actual member of the Cabinet's a Frothblower? Regrets. It's a hard life for the editor of a paper like that.'

Over a period of time it gradually emerged that

Punch was one of the factors in the world which kept Chones going, giving faith and hope. *Punch* was not on the German bookstalls, and Chones was not a man to subscribe to anything. I doubt whether he saw more than three copies during the two years of our increasing friendship in Germany. When he did, on these two or three occasions, have an actual copy in hand he would savour it in an ecstasy of pleasure. When he saw an article or drawing that struck him as funny he would shout for joy and cry 'Great! Tremendous! That's *Punch* for you!'

When there were *longeurs* his pleasure was not abated. 'They've been after *Punch* again' he would say, 'you can see where the Editor was pressured into taking out something juicy at the last minute and fill up with this stuff.'

On reading of any comical development in the social or political scene he would point it out to me and remark, 'I bet *Punch* is having a field-day with *that* this week.' And he saw the magazine not only as a clown and cabaret funny-man of superhuman wit and mordant topicality, but also as a kind of Defender of the Faith, a crusader battling in all good causes, a mighty hammerer of the Philistines, a last, lone light in the world's darkness.

'*Punch* won't let him get away with that,' he said to me once in reference to some threat of Hitler's. And again, when President Roosevelt had incurred his disapproval he comforted himself with the thought that 'if he doesn't watch his step he'll have *Punch* after him'. Nor did mistaken tendencies in religion, education, or the entire sphere of economics bother Chones unduly. *Punch* would put a spoke in the wheel of the wrongdoers—Frothblower types to a man.

I did once suggest that if *Punch* were to live fully up to the level assumed by Chones, it would need to run to about 300 pages weekly. 'I know.' he said. 'That's a difficulty. There's the paper ring, of course. Withholding supplies. But don't worry. *Punch*'ll beat them yet.'

When I started writing for *Punch* myself I found the memory of my dear friend Chones both humbling and inspiring. I and fellow-workers agreed that we could but seldom, perhaps, produce in fact material quite equal to the stuff that Chones' dreams were made of. But *Punch* always represents a sustained and rare enough effort to be worthy of the faith of all the Chones's.

CLAUD COCKBURN

CONTENTS

CONTENTS

CONTENTS

Get Set

IF I had a son who was toying with the idea of becoming a septuagenarian and wanted to know how I, who have been one now for some considerable time, felt about it, I am not sure if I should encourage him or try to throw cold water on the scheme. It is a state of life that has its drawbacks. You cannot help feeling, as the years go on, that the whole thing is getting rather silly. It seems absurd that anyone as young and sprightly as yourself should have reached such an age. You resent the stiffening of the limbs which causes you, when rising from an armchair, to remind the beholder, if a man who has travelled in Equatorial Africa, of a hippopotamus heaving itself up from the mud of a river bank. And it is annoying when taxi drivers after nearly running you down shout, "Watch it, grandpa". It was all this sort of thing that Methuselah had in mind when, interviewed by a representative of the local paper on how it felt to be nine hundred, he said, "The first hundred years are hard, but after that it's pie".

For unquestionably, once one has got the knack of it, one comes to enjoy being what Somerset Maugham calls a very old party. Ecclesiastes speaks of the evil days when the years draw nigh and thou shalt say "I have no pleasure in them" and desire shall fail and the grasshopper become a burden, but he was notoriously a man who took the dark view and was probably writing on one of his bad mornings. I think most septuagenarians will agree with me that very few of us have any real grasshopper trouble. Our limbs, as I say, may have stiffened and no doubt the arteries are hardening a bit, but there are compensations. Life becomes more tranquil. The hot blood of the late sixties has cooled. Today when I see a sexagenarian—J. B. Priestley, as it might be,

or somebody like that—climbing a tree, I smile and say to myself "Boys will be boys". "When you are my age, child," I say to myself, "you will realize that the true pleasures are mental". I am seventy-six and may quite easily go to par, and I find that I am happy just sitting and thinking, or at any rate sitting. I can detach myself from the world. And if there is a better world to detach oneself from than the one in which we are living I have yet to hear of it.

The great thing about being a septuagenarian is that you can legitimately become set in your ways. I have always wanted to do this, but in the old days something was always happening to prevent it. There was never a chance of simply doing the same thing every day, seeing nobody except wives, dogs, and cats, and being able to work regular hours without interruption, as I can now that I am in the middle seventies.

One was perpetually dashing about, leaping from continent to continent, seeing editors, lunching with managers, going out on the road with shows, popping off to Hollywood, popping back to the south of France, and generally behaving more like the jack rabbit of the prairies than anything human.

There is, of course, the possibility of getting too set in one's ways. One recalls the story of the old gentleman of regular habits who was accustomed to go out every morning to the same stationer's shop and buy his daily paper. At first the stationer would offer a word on the weather, but it was always received in silence. The old gentleman liked to walk in, pick up his paper and walk out again without speaking.

This went on for some nine years, and then the stationer moved to a larger shop on the other side of the street, and his old shop was taken by a confectioner. Knowing his client's prejudice in favour of silence, the stationer made no mention to him of the impending change, and on the morning after the confectioner had moved in the creature of habit left his house as usual, turned in at the confectioner's to buy his paper, and dropped in a heap on the floor. It seems evident that when, pottering in, he saw a tray of bath buns where for nine years he had been seeing national newspapers, their sudden impact was too much for him.

The regular life which you are able to lead in the seventies can be very pleasant after the hurly-burly of youth is over. Take mine, for instance. I rise of a morning, shave, bathe, do my Daily Dozen, have breakfast, work till lunch, take a brisk walk accompanied by a dog and two cats, work again till dinner, after dinner read a suspense novel, watch television for an hour, and so to bed. Day after day, with no variation. Monotonous? Not a bit of it. I love it. The cry goes round Remsenburg, Long Island, where I live, "Wodehouse is sitting pretty".

And a septuagenarian, mind you, is not expected to go to parties. The thought that I shall never have to wear a paper hat again is very sustaining.

So, on the whole, weighing this against that, I think that if my son were really bent on becoming a septuagenarian I should be in favour of his having a bash at it, and I would be able to give him a useful tip or two.

"George," I would say to him if his name was George, though of course 'Aneurin' if his name was Aneurin, "as far as it is within your power, stay away from the society of your juniors, and if you find yourself in such society, keep as quiet as you can, for what you have to bear in mind is that there is practically nothing you can say that will not bore the lads stiff. When watching a match at Lord's, for instance, the temptation to speak of the golden age of cricket, with special reference to Reggie Spooner's off-drive, will be very strong, but resist it.

"At the theatre, too, Irving and Dan Leno are subjects better avoided, as are *The Belle of New York* and the *Florodora* Sextette. In fact any remark beginning with the words 'Ah, but you should have seen——' should be swallowed before it can get out. The ideal septuagenarian is one who, like myself, sits in a corner and contributes absolutely nothing to the conversation. It has been well said of me by those who have seen me at social gatherings that I look like something stuffed by a good taxidermist, but nobody has ever been known to leap away from me like a startled fawn, fearing a soliloquy on the good old days.

A thing I forgot to mention, when speaking of the compensations of being a very old party, is that by the time you reach the seventies you have become more tolerant. Your kid of sixty-eight is full of juvenile prejudices, but we septuagenarians are able to take the broader, kindlier view. We accept people like Colonel Nasser and John Gordon of the *Sunday Express* as part of the great plan, knowing that they must have been put into the world for some purpose, though with our finite minds we cannot understand what that purpose was. Perhaps, we feel, we are not meant to understand.

So, on the whole, as I said before, I have no objection to being seventy-six. Fortunately, perhaps, for there seems nothing I can do about it.

P. G. WODEHOUSE

Come on, Monica, do it Again

ONE of the nicest men I ever knew used to stand an empty wine bottle upside down on a sheet of newspaper and challenge people he had only just met to take the paper away without touching or upsetting the bottle. At all ordinary times he was a decent, modest, sensible sort of chap, but the spectacle of half a dozen flushed faces topped by paper hats had him clearing a space on the table in an instant. "You just keep banging the table with one hand," he would say, "and each time you bang you give the paper a gentle pull with the other. That was a bit too hard, but you see the idea?"

Everybody saw the idea, but that did not prevent this suddenly debased werewolf from standing the bottle up on its neck again and restarting from the middle of the sheet. When he had finally brought it off he used to look round at his audience in a way that made one feel that his normal likeable three-hundred-and-sixty-four-days-in-a-year self was just a sickening pose. The revelation was so shocking that more than once I have been tempted to take the bottle and crack my old friend's head open with it.

I never actually did it, though, because some girl always got the bottle first and placing her two hands round its shoulders, if I make myself clear, bent down until the bottle was resting on the floor. In this inelegant posture, arched over like a hoop and with her hair flopping over her eyes like a sheepdog's, she would call for an empty matchbox to be set between her teeth. "What you have to do," this earnest broad-beamed object would tell us, "is to see how far you can stretch yourself out by kind of humping the bottle forward and the winner is the person who drops the matchbox furtherest away from their feet. You try it, Pam, only you ought to have your heels against the wall actually."

The devil of it is that one thing leads to another. Nobody has an empty matchbox to give the girl until he has tipped the contents out on the table, and I need hardly stress the consequences of that. The longest interval ever recorded between the emptying out of a boxful of matches and the arrangement of twelve of them by some exhibitionist into four equal squares is one and a half minutes. After

that all you have to do is to remove three matches and replace them in such a way as to make three equal squares. The hardest thing about this problem is to decide whether it is worse not to know how to do it and have to fiddle about endlessly in an interested way, or to know how to do it and have to pretend to fiddle about in order not to be a spoilsport.

There is generally a fresh-faced man with a moustache who knows how to bridge a wineglass with three matches on the cantilever principle, and the introduction of wineglasses gives Monica her chance to fill one to the brim with water and pick it up off the floor without spilling a drop while sitting on a chair with her hands tied behind her back. Good old Monica! But for her spirited example young James might never have shown us his standing spring over the sofa; and it was that splendid leap, with all the good-natured emulation to which it led, that really got the party going. Not everybody, naturally, can do a single-handed short-arm balance like Edgar, but Pam is as good as ever at swallowing lighted cigarettes, and Christopher seems to think nothing of sticking pins in his thigh. "The secret is to keep the muscles absolutely taut," he explains. Or is it absolutely loose? No matter, sit down every-one and watch. Mr Barnett is about to remove his waistcoat without taking off his jacket.

Meanwhile, reader, what of you and me? Is it conceivable that we should be content to be the beneficiaries of so much fun and skill and ingenuity and ourselves contribute nothing original to the common pool? Are we to hang our heads like boobies when appealed to, mumbling that un-fortunately one has never been much—there was a clever trick with string only it is a long time—so if they *don't* mind . . . ?

H. F. ELLIS

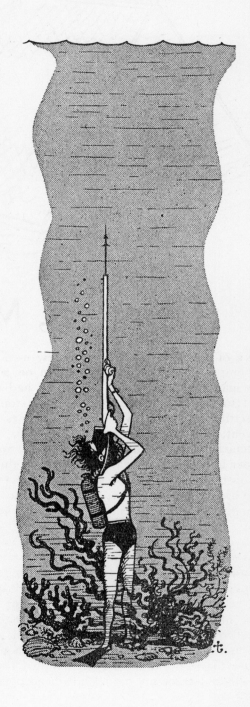

Warning to Investors

UNLESS you have money to spare
    For risky financial adventures
My earnest advice is, Beware
    Of buying Space-Travel Debentures.
Remember the Roads of Iron—
    They also began with a "Rocket,"
And today, in spite of Sir Brian,
    Are deplorably out of pocket.

E. V. MILNER

Cock House at Westminster

As Philip stepped shyly from his taxi the driver gave him a reassuring smile. "You'll soon settle down, sir," he said kindly. "I've brought many a young gentleman up on his first day at Westminster, and they all feel a bit strange at first."

Unstrapping Philip's tuckbox the cabby gave him a parting word of advice: "Keep an ear cocked for them Division Bells, and step lively when they ring—else you'll have the Whips on your tail." With a friendly nod he drove away—leaving our young friend standing uncertainly in the quadrangle.

As he waited on the threshold of his new life something of the old place's atmosphere communica-ted itself to Philip—reminding him of those others who had stood there before him, with the same pounding heart and high hopes for the future. Of all the famous company, only one—Horatio Bottomley —had turned out to be a rotter. Philip's eyes misted over as he recalled his father's parting words of advice.

The old man's face had softened, belying the gruffness of his voice, as he placed an arm round Philip's shoulders. "Remember what it's costing me to send you to Westminster, get your head down in the Divisions—and *shove*."

Squaring his shoulders at the memory of his

father's words, Philip wondered what lay in store for him during the years ahead. A seat, perhaps, on one of the television panels, or maybe an invitation to write an article about the Empire for the *Sunday Express*—Fleet Street's famous "Trumpeter". Philip had never understood how a newspaper which printed such ripping leaders—all about how splendid it was to be British and watch the flowers grow—could tolerate a fellow like Crossbencher, who wrote those sneering articles about the chaps.

But this was an unpleasant train of thought—and unpleasant thoughts should have no place on such a day as this. With a quick shrug of distaste Philip was just about to pick up his suitcase when he was hailed by a fat boy with a round, jolly face. "I say," said the fat boy, "you look like a new bug. Whose house are you in?"

"Gaitskell's," replied Philip shyly, unable to repress a thrill of pride as he spoke the famous name.

"I'm in Macmillan's," said the fat boy excitedly. "We're Cock House this term—and likely to be for a jolly long time. I'm in Suez Dorm," he added importantly, "with Bellringer Hailsham and all the other swells".

Just then a loud clanging sound rang through the building, and soon the corridors were full of boys who laughed and hostled each other as they hurried along past Philip and his friend.

As the last flying figure vanished round a bend in the corridor the fat boy turned to Philip. "Divisions!" he cried gaily. "Come and see the fun." And together they hurried off in the wake of all the others.

Philip's heart began to pound. So already he was about to witness one of the famous debates . . . perhaps even take part in one himself. He wondered what the debate was about, and decided to ask his new-found friend.

"Privileges," said the fat boy, who was hurrying along at his side. "Some rotter's been caught treading on the grass and they're going to decide what to do with him."

Seeing Philip's puzzled expression, the fat boy went on to explain that only prefects were allowed to walk across the grass: it was a privilege which they guarded jealously. Any lesser being who was found placing his beastly little foot on this hallowed ground was liable to the most fearful penalties. "Hurry," said the fat boy breathlessly, "Butcher's making a maiden".

Philip went scarlet in the face. This, he felt certain, was what his father had warned him about. At the time he had not been sure of his father's meaning when the old man had said "One day, you'll meet the woman you want to marry—but she won't want you if you've been rolling in the mud—like Tanbark there". And the general had waved a stick angrily at one of his hounds.

"H—how do you mean, sir?" Philip had stammered nervously, certain that he was treading on dangerous ground.

The general cleared his throat noisily. "Hrrmph. In my day at Westminster some of the fellows used to lark about with the maids—kissin' and all that rot. Devilish bad for the character and even worse for the wind. Keep clear of it, is my advice to you."

That was what his father had said, and already—on his first day at Westminster—Philip was being invited to watch this fellow Butcher rotting about. The hot blood mounted Philip's face until it was crimson to the roots of his hair.

Before he could say anything the fat boy motioned him to a halt. They had reached their destination—the huge room in which was being debated the motion " . . . That this House always hopes for the Best, while retaining the right to fear the Worst".

A tall, distinguished-looking boy was just rising to speak when a shrill voice from the other side of the house shouted the single word: "Resign!" Instantly the cry was taken up in a deep-throated chorus which echoed round the room. Philip's eyes shone—all his earlier fears forgotten—as he contemplated the turbulent scene. "How simply ripping!" he breathed.

Suddenly he found that he was shouting wildly himself. "*Resign!*" "*Withdraw!*" and "*Shame . . .!*" The words tumbled eagerly from his lips. As heads turned approvingly in his direction, Philip felt a little thrill of pride. Westminster had accepted him.

A tug upon his sleeve interrupted Philip's thoughts—and, turning, he found the fat boy's eyes fixed pleadingly upon his own. "I say," said his companion, "let's you and me be friends".

Thrilled by the events of a crowded day, Philip gladly agreed. So, arm in arm and happily paired, the two friends went down to the tuckshop for tea.

STUART McKIBBIN

*　　*　　*

"Lady Sarah Craven, 18, . . . spent part of the past summer working in a holiday camp—cutting sandwiches. Next month she hopes to start training as a manicurist."

Sunday Express

Thanks for the warning.

Slay Your Own Dragon

A rousing St George's Day appeal to the youth of England to live in the spirit of the illustrious Patron Saint.

IT was St George himself who was put to death on April 23, not the dragon, although to be honest little more is known about the one than the other. There is a school that believes St George to have been a grocer of Cappadocia. He became an army contractor ("What's for dinner? Dragon *again?*") and a tax-gatherer and finally Archbishop of Alexandria, a promotion equally rare today in both NAAFI and the Inland Revenue. Also it is quite possible that the Saint was not martyred by Diocletian at Nicomedia on April 23, 303, but at Lydda in 250, give or take a few years. There are even ill-disposed folk who claim that it was not St George at all that slew the dragon (who first appeared in *The Golden Legend* in 1275) but Perseus. The rock from which Perseus delivered Andromeda by slaying a monster was at Joppa (now the Jaffa Sporting Club), only a short bus-ride from Lydda (now Lydda), where St George lived.

Be all this as it may, St George has exactly the right characteristics for an English national saint, and his example is a splendid one for young people, in whom the dragon-slaying instinct seems to be lying fallow at the moment.

It is no good arguing that the younger generation doesn't have a fair chance because no one will supply them with any dragons. St George did not sit in his office waiting for people to bring a dragon to his door and ask him to slay it for them. In point of fact he had to go all the way to Silene in Libya, where there was a dragon inhabiting a pool, and the Princess Sabra—well, suppose we go back a stage: it seems there was this dragon, whose normal ration was two sheep a day, not an unreasonable diet, one would have said, for a beast requiring all those extra calories for the smoke and fire. But the locals ran out of sheep and the dragon had to be fed on human beings; and villagers being what they are it was no time at all before they ran so low on those too that Princess Sabra found herself requisitioned as the *plat du jour*.

It was at this stage that St George appeared. His

KNOW YOUR ENEMY. Top, *the Mark I dragon as slain by St George.* Centre, *the Mark II, as modified for Chinese service, with increased cruising-speed and hotter breath.* Bottom, *the Mark IV dragon with triple warhead, still operating in comparatively saintless areas.*

Recommended position for slaying dragons of all early types. Note firm seat and strong grip on lance. The lance is the special long anti-dragon model enabling the slayer to keep well clear of the dragon's breath.

methods are worthy of attention. He did not slay the dragon outright, but only wounded it to such an extent that it submitted to being led back to the village on the end of the princess's girdle. Not until St George was sure of a good house did he administer the final *coup de grâce*.

So it is clear that no young Englishman can expect to meet, let alone slay, a dragon simply by sitting in his bed-sitter like Jimmy Porter, bleating "How I long for a little human enthusiasm," or for a dragon if that is what he really thinks he wants. The problem today is three-fold:

(1) where to look for dragons,
(2) how to recognize them when seen,
(3) how to slay them.

Real dragons of flesh, blood and fire have almost died out, having for the most part been slain by saints. Even in China, where they lingered on until quite recently, their numbers have been drastically reduced by the Mao regime in its relentless pursuit of vermin. The best dragons to go for nowadays are intangible, such as were referred to by Thomas Moore—

In England the garden of beauty is kept
   By a dragon of prudery placed within call.

Prudery is quite a modest dragon, though a bit of slaying would do it no harm. A most savage dragon called Intolerance has long ago finished its sheep-ration and is hungering for human sacrifices. There is a nauseating new dragon called Senti-

Below are shown various methods of giving the coup de grâce. The left-hand diagram illustrates the classic, or Royal St George, method, with the head sliced cleanly off at the neck. In the centre is an alternative method for use on dragons with extra-tough necks. The right-hand diagram shows an interesting if rather flashy variant of this for use in front of large audiences.

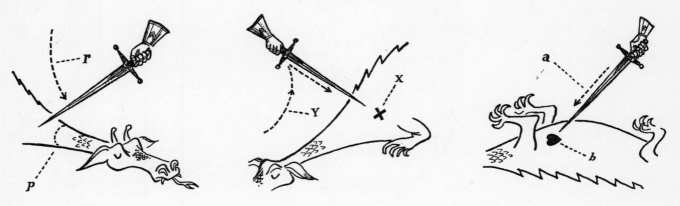

19

mentality, which eats kiddies, doggies, old folk and the physically handicapped, and spits them out into the pages of the daily newspapers and the Light Programme. Other dragons worth slaying are Juvenile Delinquency, H-bomb, and Racial Conflict.

There is also a dragon on the Welsh flag, but this is only a symbolical one put there to remind the Welsh of their bad luck in not having St George for their patron saint.

Slaying contemporary dragons, as you can see, is not so simple a matter as St George had to do with. However, the broad principles still work. One of them is, never go for the dragon while it is still in the sheep-eating stage. Wait until there is a princess on the verge of sacrifice and then rush in; you will earn the plaudits and the thanks of everyone, instead of angry expostulations like "You cruel thing, why can't you leave it alone? It's not doing you any harm, is it?"

Remember also this business about wounding the dragon first and then leading it back to where the press cameras are. The object of this is not simply to get yourself extra publicity; it is to give your princess, or whoever is representing her, a share of the credit, and also to make sure that people believe your claim. If you dispatch your dragon in the middle of the desert there will not be lacking envious people who will allege that the beast had actually died of foot-and-mouth or an over-heated firebox or some cause equally natural, and was already dead when you found it.

B. A. YOUNG

'Oh—about here, I should think.'

Sunset and Sunrise

The sun that sinks
Is subtler than one thinks,
Expanding what the daylight shrinks,
And flooding all the world in sombre inks.
It is more apt than half a dozen different drinks
To make the tree a troll, the bush a bear, the log a lynx,
The signal light a star, the garden shed the shadow of the Sphinx.

The sun that rises
Sobers and yet surprises.
The world casts off its dark disguises;
Objects stand forth again their proper sizes,
Freed from the wild dimensions that the mind devises—
Yet the mind questions, while it relishes what reason prizes:
Is this the truth, or that? Day's certainties, or suspect night's surmises?

R. P. LISTER

'Isn't it time we went, dear? I think this gentleman's ready for bed.'

ШЕРПОК ГОПМЕС

The Immortal Sleuth of 22IB Baku Street

Two million roubles, I gather, are being claimed from Russian publishers for recent profits from the works of the late Sir Arthur Conan Doyle, "the creator of Sherlock Holmes". So says *The Times*.

I don't know whether this would have astounded Dr Watson. It astounds me. The Dreaming Musician, the Skilled Scientist, the Arch-Investigator, in spite of some rather foolish statements made by his medical friend, was also a violent political propagandist, and his political studies wherever they led him were not scarlet in hue. Hear him in *The Adventure of the Noble Bachelor*:

"It is always a joy to me to meet an American, Mr Moulton, for I am one of those who believe that the folly of a monarch and the blundering of a Minister in far-gone years will not prevent our children from being some day citizens of the same world-wide country under a flag which shall be a quartering of the Union Jack with the Stars and Stripes."

I do not seem to hear this prophecy bubbling lightly from Nikita Khrushchev's lips, nor echoed by any member of the Soviet Præsidium. Even in the England of 1892, when it first appeared in print, it may have been a rather daring anticipation. But Lord Robert Walsingham de Vere St Simon, formerly Under Secretary for the Colonies, had left the room when the words were spoken. He took no part in that supper of "cold woodcock, pheasant, *paté de foie gras* pie with a group of ancient and cobwebby bottles" which graced the reunion of Hetty Doran and her transatlantic spouse. And the integration of the British Commonwealth with the United States of America still remains, curiously enough, unconsummated.

> The stately Holmes of England
> How beautiful he stands
> The muscles of his brawny arms
> Are strong as iron bands.

I don't remember who wrote that, but a more endearing aspect of his character, in Russian eyes, may be his contempt for the British aristocracy. Lord St Simon was the second son of the Duke of Balmoral ("Hum! Arms: Azure, three caltrops in chief over a fess sable"). He inherited Plantagenet blood by direct descent, and Tudor on the distaff side. ("Ha! Well, there is nothing very instructive in all this.") And in fact he is treated with ridicule throughout the whole story. It is my surmise that Lord Backwater was his elder brother, and it was Lord Backwater who, in *The Adventure of Silver Blaze*, employed as his trainer a man of whom Holmes remarked, as Watson and they trudged along together, "A more perfect compound of the bully, coward and sneak than Master Silas Brown I have seldom met with".

23

And what of the Beryl Coronet? Whose was "that name which is a household word all over the earth— one of the highest, noblest, most exalted names in England"? Who was it who placed in pawn "one of the most precious public possessions of the Empire" to satisfy an immediate financial need?

But these were mere domestic adventurings. All round the globe ranged the political manœuvres of the man who slew Moriarty at the Reichenbach Falls. It was he who penetrated the colossal scandal of the Baron Maupertuis, in connection with the Netherland Sumatra Company. It was he who looked in at Mecca, visited Lhasa, and rendered assistance to the Khalifa of Khartoum. How does that fit in with the Party Line of the Union of Soviet Socialist Republics? Most surely this man was a colonial meddler, a bloodthirsty agent of capitalist intrigues.

Finally, if you please, he was "summoned to Odessa to unravel the Trepoff Murder". What does your young Ukrainian reader make of that, I should like to know? Not an atom secret would have baffled the great Western warmonger for longer than a pipeful of shag, nor is there any corner of Siberia that he would not with his microscope have explored. None the less:

> *The stately Holmes of England*
> *How beautiful he stands*
> *Beyond the Iron Curtain*
> *In Byelorussian lands.*

And doubtless he will go farther still. Very likely before these words are printed *The Hound of the Baskervilles* will have become a text-book for students in Peking.

EVOE

'Golly! . . . they're still thirsty! . . .'

24

Directive

(King's Cross Station is to be "scrapped and completely rebuilt." No doubt the finished work will take its tone from the Continental Sun Terrace opened recently on Platform 13 at Euston.)

From: **The Chairman, Railway Executive**

To: **Stationmaster, King's Croissant**

MEMBERS of the Executive desire me to convey to you their cordial good wishes for the successful discharge of your duties, which you assume fully with the opening of the Station on Monday next.

2. You will have studied the *Transport (Amendment) (Continentalization of Amenities) Act*, 1967, and thus become conversant with the broader legal aspects. My concern in this *directive* is to emphasize certain of these aspects, and to ensure, by touching on some subordinate matters, that the proud name of the Executive shall lose nothing, and gain much, by (so to say) the *initiative* of its *syndicat*.

3. GAMING ROOMS

(*a*) In the Public Room (opp. Platform 9), as you know, the permitted games are three only, roulette, baccarat and trente-et-quarante. I think we must take it that this rules out the passenger who uses the rooms to complete football coupons or enter newspaper competitions. Later a *boule* game may be sanctioned, which may be more to the taste of this type of player. In the meantime, offenders should not be treated too brusquely. A reading from the Act should suffice,

together with an invitation to participate in one of the legitimate games. In the event of trouble, the Railway Police have been briefed on their powers under the Gaming (*Amendment*) (*Passengers Awaiting Trains*) *Acts*.

(*b*) In the Private Room (or *Salle Privée*, as it will say on the duty porter's hat), the variety of games is wider, and will include craps. Evening dress is obligatory, except in the case of U.S. servicemen commissioned and in uniform.

(*c*) Passports will not be required, a valid ticket being sufficient as an admitting document, provided it is not:

   (i) A platform ticket;

   (ii) A cheap-day ticket,

   (iii) A dog, bicycle, or similar ticket. Second-class ticket-holders will be allowed in the Public Room only.

4. SWIMMING

There are three *bains*, all with *plages*, and though bathers will be warned that the Executive can accept no responsibility for trains lost by thoughtless bathers, all three will be within convenient view of the station announcer's box, and a system of coloured trunks and/or caps, representing trains leaving in a quarter-hour, half-hour, hour, etc., will enable the colours to be "called" over the loudspeaker system. Passengers will be expected to adjust their clothes before leaving unless they have reserved sleeping compartments, in which case they may board the *train* direct from the *bain*.

Note.—Loudspeaker warning must be given at all times of electricity failure, as the temperature of the water will drop sharply.

5. RESTAURANTS

(*a*) The amenities for eating, drinking and (artificial) sun-bathing are regarded by the Executive as the project's *pièce de résistance*, and it is intended that the full resources of the Hotels and Catering Department shall be made available. Manpower remains a problem, however, and in seconding railwaymen from other duties to serve as waiters, chefs, gipsy violinists, etc., care must be taken to interfere with the business of the Railway as little as possible. Train crews, for instance, should if possible remain intact. Voluntary courses have been instituted for those interested in work as *restaurateurs*, and may be taken *in railway time* at the following centres:

   (i) Tea-room, Marylebone

   (ii) Euston Hotel

   (iii) Great Eastern Hotel (Liverpool Street)

   (iv) The Buffet, Victoria (closed)

   (v) North British Station Hotel, Edinburgh

   (vi) The Canteen, 222 Marylebone Road, N.W.1.

Each course will include a grounding in menu French, thus enabling waiters to explain what fare is being offered.

(*b*) The Station's inventory includes three hundred and eighty coloured, *plage*-type umbrellas in striped plastic, most of which should be allocated to the restaurants. Every effort should be made to keep these free from grease and soot. Particles of grit, etc., can render the daintiest *gâteau* unappetizing.

(*c*) Tea-bags are to be used *once only*.

Note.—Hotels Executive Reg. 2018 (k) xxiv. (M) may be taken as amended accordingly.

(d) Drivers operating from Platform 7, on which is sited *L'Espresso au Cheapday* (*casses-croûtes* only), should be instructed not to blow off steam when the wind is in the west.

(e) The Executive has undertaken as far as possible to meet the wishes of the Musicians' Union with regard to excessive shunting and whistling in the vicinity of Restaurants where orchestras will play.

6. TONE TO BE MAINTAINED

(a) Commensurate with efficient running of the Railway, which must not be allowed to fall below its traditional high standard, no effort should be spared to maintain the Continental flavour at which the Executive's planners have aimed throughout. It is thought that excesses have been on the whole avoided; female attendants will not, for example, be placed in charge of gentlemen's conveniences, as is the custom on the other side of the Channel; even so, and bearing in mind that passengers from the North and Midlands will be in preponderance, there is some danger that, in the early stages, an unsympathetic or even ribald attitude may be adopted towards less familiar amenities. Railway Police are *not* empowered to make arrests in such cases as

(i) Feet placed on tables,

(ii) Tea-dregs, bottles, etc., placed in fountains,

(iii) Caps worn during meals.

There may, however, occur breaches of civil law chargeable as wilful damage or public nuisance, *e.g.*,

(iv) Scribbling on or otherwise defacing caryatids or other statuary or ornamentation the property of the Executive,

(v) Converting menus, wine-lists, etc., into paper boats to float in the *bains*,

In this event, action can and should be taken.

26

(*b*) Without prejudice to anything laid down in (*a*) above, police should be encouraged in reasonable indulgence towards genuine Continental behaviour by genuine Continentals. It is the Executive's hope that French, Italian, and other foreigners will be attracted by the "home-from-home" atmosphere, and to discourage them from a return visit would be unfortunate. For example, innocent slaps at a passing waitress should not be taken to constitute an offence.

7. AMENITIES, ATTENTION TO BE DRAWN TO

(*a*) It has happened in the past that the Executive's best efforts have gone for nothing owing to the passenger's ignorance of their existence. (In 1956-7 only three dog's-bed tickets were sold.) This must not be allowed to occur in the present case. All that is possible will be done by the Public Relations Department. The following posters in full colour have already been printed (1,000,000 of each):

   (i) THE CÔTE D'AZUR for 9*s*. 6*d*. RETURN!

   (ii) GET A BRITISH RAILWAYS TAN!

   (iii) C'EST MERVEILLEUX, BA GOOM!

8. In conclusion, the Executive desire me to convey to you their confidence and high hopes for your success in this vital assignment. For myself I would add only three final reminders:

   (i) There will be no Sunday opening.

   (ii) All amenities to close one hour after sunset, Greenwich Mean Time.

   (iii) Our first annual Battle of Flowers is provisionally scheduled for April 1st, 1979.

September 17th, 1978
      LIEUT.-GEN. *J. B. Boothroyd*
             CHAIRMAN.

'*Do you think you could find someone to suit my wife?*'

Cover Story

GOLD paint used to be what you couldn't stop touching up the house with once you'd started. Now it's that plastic paper with the tear-off back. Plain, spotted, striped, sprigged and the same price whatever the trade-mark. Buy a yard in a dainty pastel green. Work your thumbnail into a corner and pull, revealing adhesive surface. Quick! What wants to *be* a dainty pastel green *and* heatproof, smearproof, wipeable with damp cloth? That kitchen cabinet! Slap your Plastostick down its disgusting plain grey side. If placed crooked the stuff can be torn away and replaced straight. Better the first time, wasn't it? *And* the second! Smooth out air-bubbles and before applying to other side, front and drawers, for heaven's sake clean old surface and allow to dry.

Now you have a dainty green kitchen cabinet instead of a dainty grey one. Think this over fully—remember the American who took five years to train a flamingo and all he had at the end was a trained flamingo—before you rush out and buy your next six yards of red-and-white striped Colorgay.

Kitchen drawers lined with red-and-white striped Colorgay take on a new lease of life. Cocoa tins covered with it look like biscuit tins, which look like covered cocoa tins. Larder shelves look gay and workmanlike, pussy's margarine box just looks gay and she won't go near it now. Windowsills look so festive and proof against wet flowerpot saucers that you can't think how you ever had a plain sill in your house!

Or a plain skirting-board, desk-top, *Children's Encyclopædia*, spare-room ceiling or corkscrew-handle! Easy on the purple-spotted acid-yellow with that little suitcase—hubby takes it to the office! And honestly, if the Eezi-Adheezo makers had wanted to provide you with black-and-white check bathroom curtains wouldn't they just have left the sticky part *off* rather than give you the trouble of clamping two bits . . .

Oh, and you know the tool cupboard where you keep the creosote? Well, the tin leaks. And that brown jelly you'll find *under* the creosote, that was Eezi-Adheezo too, only this morning. Must be something in plastic and creosote the same, some constituent, mustn't there, or something?

Never mind. Home experts tell us that *the* new stuff for cupboard and drawers is newspaper, so easy to lay—and to replace, they add, if you hang on to your *Sunday Times* Magazine Section!

ANGELA MILNE

A Question of Taste

O SPLENDOUR of slenderness, beautiful ghost!
With your suitable fruit and your terrible toast,
Do you yearn to return to the tart and the pie
And your fill of the grill and the roast and the fry?
Or do you believe you achieve all you wish
Not by cooking, but *looking*, a sumptuous dish?

HAZEL TOWNSON

You Too Can be an Author

MANY people think how wonderful it would be to go into bookshops and see their books in shining piles. What puts them off is the completely unfounded belief that producing enough words to keep the covers apart is impossible for the normally constituted man, a delusion due to the ordinary, clean-living Englishman's vagueness about literary length. This article, for example, will come out at about nine hundred words, give or take a few. Write one a week and in a year and a half you have a book the length of the average lightish novel.

Of course, to many literary men the idea of doing only nine hundred words a week would be preposterous. So would the idea of producing only one book in eighteen months. Sir Compton Mackenzie has said he can do a novel in two months. Mr John Creasey, who has as many pen-names as most novelists have characters, at the age of forty-nine has produced nine hundred and fifty books. He said to the *Sunday Express*, "I write each book in about a week and revise it in another three days. I have lots of free time." It is true his books are only sixty thousand words, but he has produced a total of some thirty-five million words already. Simenon's procedure is to have his blood-pressure taken, write most of his time for eleven days and have his blood-pressure taken again. Edgar Wallace used to dictate night and day until he finished a book. Then he went to bed and slept until it was time to go to the races.

Some time ago there was a puzzling news item about Mr John Masters who was said to write twenty thousands words a day with the aid of an electric typewriter. I do not quite see how the electricity would help you to think what to say; but perhaps he had thought of that already. After all, Mr Masters does not write very many books, unless he too goes

29

in for pseudonyms. Perhaps he walks about enjoying life and making it all up and then discharges his cargo in occasional binges. Gibbon used to compose in his head and then just act as his own amanuensis. Perhaps if he had had an electric quill he would not have needed twenty years for the *Decline and Fall*. While I am showing how little time authorship takes I might go on to mention that Wells never worked after breakfast; that Miss Denise Robins has just had time to open a church fete and tell a reporter that she has scored one hundred and seventeen novels; and that Dickens would often go off on holiday for months at a time.

To feed the fantasy still further let me point out that if your typewriter is not wired for electricity you can hire a tape-recorder and get your novel transcribed at a cost that should easily be covered by the publisher's advance. Listen to a B.B.C. talk and see how slowly it goes. Surely you could keep up that speed as you speak into the machine. After all, the man who talks about Persia or Inflation has to find facts and repeat them correctly, while you are not bound by anything and if your characters begin to do things you cannot describe fluently you just make them do something else. The official B.B.C. rate of speech for talks—not, of course, for patter comedians —is one thousand eight hundred words in a quarter of an hour. That is, seven thousand two hundred per hour. You need not hire the tape-recorder for more than one day! If you begin after breakfast, say nine o'clock, with threequarters of an hour for lunch and a quarter of an hour for tea you would have enough words for a novel that would actually be

longer than Mr Creasey's crime stories before eight o'clock. Here is another encouraging calculation. Say a gossipy letter covers three sides of paper, call it five hundred words. A letter a day for five days a week would produce a seventy-five thousand novel in thirty weeks.

But, you may object, what about Flaubert? Didn't Conrad sometimes take ten hours over a page? Doesn't Mr Graham Greene take two years over a novel, not a very long one? Didn't Virginia Woolf say two hours a day was the most a writer should write for? I had been talking about quantity and here you are dragging quality in. However, look at the man who seems to prove anything in any argument about literature, Henry James.

James was the most subtle, the most discriminating, the most hard-thinking of writers. He spent hours in elaborate conversations. He kept his friendships in repair and had endless time for acquaintanceships. The common picture of him is of a writer who was precious, complex, almost sterile. He dictated, but from behind a curtain. Yet in libraries the shelves of James go on and on. The volumes are fat ones. Their type is close set. What is more, he sat down to revise his published novels and republished them in fresh and much elaborated versions. Every few months they seem to dig up another couple of volumes of hitherto uncollected magazine articles or even regular newspaper journalism. He wrote long and frequent letters. He kept notebooks. As far as productivity went he was far nearer to Mr Creasey than he was to the stereotype of a "serious literary artist." But then so were Dickens and Shakespeare.

R. G. G. PRICE

'My compliments to the chef.'

'... Silvery mo-o-o-on, we're gonna hit you so-o-o-on.'

John Higgins

JOHN HIGGINS was a councillor of credit and renown,
　　Who was more than proud to represent his ward.
He had read his party handbook and the story of his town,
　　And he wore the smartest suits he could afford.

He loved his Mother Country, and he loved his Fellow Men,
　　And Tradition, and the Individual Choice;
Broad-mindedly, he loved the other party now and then,
　　And was partial to his own official voice.

He trod the path of reason at the Rotary debate,
　　But of dogma when he took the party line,
Of humility on Sunday when he took around the plate,
　　And of pride when seen upstanding, taking wine.

For all the decent principles worth standing for, he stood;
　　If committees needed sitting on, he sat.
He crowned a public lifetime in the cause of public good
　　By acceptance of the chain and tricorn hat.

John Higgins was a councillor who made himself a name,
　　And fulfilled a useful purpose—let's be fair—
But he did so for the reason that he revelled in the game,
　　So must we have his statue in the square?

DAVID PROCKTER

32

Singing in the Rain

YELLOW grass grew thinly on shale slopes like hair on black scalps. Scrawny sheep, down from dirty mountains, stumbled over scrap-iron dumps, stood uncertainly outside signal boxes, browsed on the asphalt of deserted playgrounds. It was Bank Holiday, but two miles of steelworks smoked, flamed and stank like Sunday.

Under webs of sodden bunting, crowds converged on the Royal National Eisteddfod pavilion. This is of timber and corrugated metal, seats eight thousand and looks like a mammoth freight store. Every year it is taken down and carted to a new site. At Ebbw Vale it had been re-erected on a levelled-off mine tip. From its ceiling hung trays of television crews and cameras. An organ made holy rumbles; its console, alongside the platform, was in the sort of glossy, pale wood that coffins are made of.

The Rt. Hon. Aneurin Bevan, P.C., made brief presidential appearances. White-plumed and peremptory of underlip, he sat in floodlight with his eyes focused on infinity, or anyway on the pavilion's rear wall, which is much the same thing and, except when clapping other speakers, which he did dutifully, looked not as if sitting for his bust by Epstein, but like the perfected bust itself, with pedestal, in the National Portrait Gallery.

Brass bands trooped on and off the platform. With one of these I had travelled up on the honking diesel from Cwm.

The first euphonium and the first cornet, both young and blond, wore rhinestone tiepins, ebon scarves with white filigree patterns, and metal-cloth suits in stardust weave. That is to say, their suits, like pieces of planetarium sky, were dead black and thickly asperged with silver.

I asked them who their artist-manager was and, before they could reply, told them not to trust him, adding that people who took a twopenny royalty on ten-inch 78s always ended up in the free-soup queue.

"But we're miners, we're coal-face workers, man."

"Indeed?"

"We got our stardusts from the tailor in Cwm, man, fifteen pounds apiece. You've got to order them."

"Oh, yes?"

We got out of the train in cold, floating rain. In a hillside field men were setting up little menhirs around the Loganstone and secreting microphones and loud-speakers in movable, ivy-draped oak stumps. It was going to be a wet Gorsedd, they muttered.

In a chapel vestry half a mile away, the Keeper of the Gorsedd Regalia, Mr Cotton, a youngish man with blue eyes, whitish hair and an underslung pipe, arranged three hundred Gorsedd robes on hangers.

"All back from the cleaners," he said . . . "all but one, that is. There's not a cleaner in England who'll take the Archdruid's robe. Pure silk, fifty years old (feel the weight!), fraying badly. It would come back in ribbons. So the Archdruid has to go dirty. Seen the Archdruid's crown? It's in the chest over there. Circlet of oak leaves and acorns in bronze. Very stylish, I think. Mind you don't trip over the Grand Sword. You've never seen a sword that size before, I'll bet. Bigger than the Grand Sword Bearer himself. And nearly as heavy. Here's the Hirlas Horn. Handsome, huh? 'The Hirlas Horn,' it says in the official book, 'is proffered to the Archdruid by a Matron in token of the wine of welcome'."

"The horn doesn't actually *contain* wine, then?"

Mr Cotton found this very droll. He put his pipe down, clapped his hands to his flanks and threw his head back like an innkeeper in comic opera.

Outside the rain stopped floating and became stair-rods. Switched from the soaking hillside, the Gorsedd rites were shoe-horned into a Congregational chapel. Top-flight druids jostled each other amiably in the bit of space between pulpit and communion rail while flash bulbs bloomed and waned along the edge of the gallery.

The typical druid has horn-rimmed glasses and, around the eyes, good-humoured crinkles of a special, middle-aged kind, the kind that come when a man knows, or thinks he knows, he is looked up to and loved by one and all. Under the immemorial robes of Celtic paganism, polytheism and, at a pinch, sun worship, he retains the dog-collar of his calling. For Nonconformism is one of Druidry's stouter props. He sings, orates, prays, poetizes, thinks—does everything, in fact, but pay his bills—in the Welsh language. Only two per cent of Ebbw Vale's population are Welsh-speaking. But what of that? They heard little or nothing else spoken or sung in the Eisteddfod pavilion all week. It was the Gorsedd boys who saw to that. Their edicts are as iron.

From the shiny mahogany pulpit, with its burden of great gilt-edged Bibles, a young woman with radiant eyes and green robes—those of Musician Ovate—sang what sounded to me like an Ode in Ukrainian about happy mushroom gatherers. (Really it was a hymn which likened Life to a flowing river, Youth to green valleys, and Time to a threshold on which multitudes face a happy eternity). It wasn't her eyes alone that radiated. Her voice radiated. Her whole person radiated. Altogether a splendid type of Welsh womanhood. Probably, I told myself, she was the wife of a modestly prospering Welsh farmer. . . Every week she baked Welsh cakes on an old Welsh bake-stone. Every night she sang her bairns to sleep with Welsh lullabies, self-accompanied on the Welsh harp. . . . She might have gone out into great cities, into the great world. Certainly she studied at the University College of Aberystwyth. It was there she took the degree in Welsh that qualified her for Ovateship . . . But no. She had been content to sit down among God's good mountains, drawing strength and salt for the spirit from that nurturing soil whence she and her forebears had sprung. (Observe what a few days' contact with Welsh nationalism does for one's prose). The Great Homekeeper, I would call her.

"She's the greenest thing in the Gorsedd," said a voice at my elbow, Mr Cotton's, of course. His reference was to the Great Homekeeper's robe, not to any immaturity in her singing. The green robes of the Ovates and the Bards' blue ones are among Mr Cotton's perpetual worries. "They fade like nobody's business in sunlight," he mourned.

"What's sunlight?" inquired a facetious junior herald with wet feet.

The Gorsedd broke up, shed its canvas high-boots, gorgets, cloth-of-gold dolmans. In the vestry a reporter interviewed the Great Homekeeper.

"Yes," I heard her say. "I do get around a bit. I've sung before the Queen three times, the Queen Mother twice, the Sultan of Morocco once. Next week I fly to Milan. Last time I was in the air I took my Welsh harp with me. The steward said 'Harp, madam? You're on the wrong 'plane. We don't go as far as *that*. Ho-ho-ho'."

Anybody can make a mistake. I was right about the Stardust Twins though. Before I left they were being paged in the County Hotel bars and six tea tents by a man purporting to be the social secretary of the Mynydd Llangynidr Working Men's Institute and Burial Club. Actually he was an agent from Las Vegas with a trunkful of television contracts.

CHARLES REID

34

Landladies in My Life

On balance I suppose I've been more trouble to landladies than they've been to me. Although I was undoubtedly the innocent party when the baker pitched me into the gutter of the Old Kent Road. His wife was an attentive landlady and a beautiful cook, but she had this nympho streak. She took more than a fancy to me at seventeen and was chasing me round and round the dough-bin one evening when her husband came in and caught her hot-handed. Unfortunately he got the impression, which she immediately encouraged, that I was chasing her, and he tossed me into the street forthwith.

I next found shelter with Mrs Tablet who kept me physically comfortable, but spiritually uneasy. She made a profession, a religion and a way of life out of superstition, eternally watching for omens of ill-luck and patiently seeking out their fulfilment. Spilt salt, thirteen, cross-eyes, ladders, Macbeth, tea-leaves and such bric-a-brac haunted her life, and once she had spotted a portent of doom she couldn't rest easy until she had tracked down its fruition. Sometimes, I was certain, she engineered events to fulfil a foreboding.

The floor creaked under the lino in the front passage as I came in one night. Mrs Tablet recited happily.

"When the floor creaks, within the week there'll be a broken bone."

Nobody broke any limbs in the house during the next three days, so she went into action herself. She polished the lino till it was slippery as ice and the door-mat slid like a puck. Then she reported a gas-leak and got the fitter as he stepped briskly through the front door. He was a big man and he came down like an avalanche and fractured something in his wrist. Whether it was the superstition satisfied, or his weight bashing the joists into place, I don't know, but the creaking stopped.

Her favourite superstition concerned two plaster bas-relief portraits she had of King Edward VII and Queen Alexandra. They were set in oval frames about two feet long, hung side by side on the kitchen wall, and were harbingers of death. Whenever the Reaper was coming to the house one of those pictures fell down, and the sex of the monarch indicated the sex of the next one to go. Mrs Tablet's

'I'm extremely interested in where I'm going—more than most, perhaps.'

grandmother was run over by a mineral-dray three days after Queen Alexandra hit the floor. King Edward came down one Easter Saturday and on the Bank Holiday they carried old Mr Tablet in through the front door on a builder's ladder, stark and stiff and the beer-froth still wet on his moustache. The Queen fell one Tuesday morning and Mrs Tablet's mother laughed about it; but she didn't laugh no more after the Friday because, by then, she was laid out in the bedroom and looking like an angel from heaven in the best elm-and-brass-handles money could buy. Mrs Tablet's husband, God rest his soul, but for the drink as fine a man as ever breathed and don't let me hear none as says different, went out like a light in that very chair you're sitting in four days after King Edward bumped the lino. She lost her first and her third, and both their passings were prophesied by the plaster pictures. Nobody died in that house but Edward and Alexandra gave them time to repent and make peace. So you will understand that I felt the creeping frost-bite when Mrs Tablet brought me a cup of tea one morning and asked sadly "How do you feel?"

"All right," I said. "Why?"

"King Edward. 'E come down in the night. Like a bomb it was when 'e 'it the floor. I come up and looked at you straight away, but you was still breaving."

"Why shouldn't I be breathing?"

"You're the only man in the 'ouse, ain't you? And King Edward's come down."

And she left me to my doom.

All that week she kept looking at me for signs of death.

" 'Ow you feeling, son?" she'd ask me ten times a day.

"You ain't eating much, are you? I suppose you're losing your appetite now, eh?"

I wasn't losing my appetite. I was afraid to eat except when hunger forced me. I reckoned that if I didn't kick the bucket by the end of the week she'd be after poisoning me to make King Teddy's warning come true. What I wanted was a food-taster, but I couldn't afford one on my salary as an apprentice park-keeper. When she didn't do my washing the next Monday—what was the point? I'd never need another change—I packed my bag and crept out in the middle of the night. So that she and King Edward wouldn't pursue me to the death I left a note saying I'd been crossed in love and was going to jump in the river.

I went to stay later on with a Miss Pool and she frightened me, too, in the end. Religious and happy in melancholy, she used to leave a fresh text by my porridge each morning. Her greatest pleasure was to hear of the misfortunes of others. Somebody fell off a bus, or got pneumonia, or caught in a revolving door, and Miss Pool hailed it as a triumph for divine justice, retribution to another deserving sinner.

"You only get served evil if you've lived evil," she'd say happily.

The only person she had a good word for was a bedridden Salvationist opposite who used to wear the top half of her uniform in bed and sing hymns all day. One winter's afternoon she was singing away devoutly when her roof caved in and snow and ceiling crashed all over her bed. I wondered how Miss Pool would fit the event into her tit-for-tat theory.

"Awful thing," I said. "A saintly old lady suffering an accident like that. Whatever could she have done to deserve it?"

36

"I don't know. Not yet. But there was something she had to pay for, never fear." She smiled deeply. "God don't pay his debts in money."

God don't pay his debts in money . . . I didn't know exactly what it meant but the words sent a cold wind from the river whistling straight up my shirt. To this day the sentence lurks in my subconscious and, at recollection, sends draughts blowing round my soul. When I finally knock at the tradesmen's side-entrance to the Golden Gates St Peter will look out and say "Oh! it's you, is it. Now you're going to find out, my lad. God don't pay his debts in money."

But the landlady to whom I owe my greatest debt is Mrs Murphy—or, more directly perhaps, to Mr Murphy, Nature's master of the art of writing, the Quiller-Couch of the Old Kent Road.

Everything was perfick at Mrs Murphy's—the bed, the fire, the food, the price—and I could have lived out my life at her house. A fat, cheerful soul, her face and spirit a tribute to stout, she talked from morning to night. She doted like a mother on a pet canary she kept in the front room. Gloria it was called, and it lived in a cage hung with enough tassels and trinkets to sicken a sultan.

Mr Murphy worked down the sewers and had two pairs of those enormous boots. He loved those boots the way his wife loved her canary and spent most of his spare time polishing them. He was a man of very few words and rarely spoke all day, except to ask for condiments. He sat and he smoked, and he polished and he thought.

The only time in my life any female picked me up in the street, it turned out to be a cat. It looked thin and pathetic and gave me so much of the dumb-friend malarkey that I persuaded Mrs Murphy to let me keep it in the house on my solemn promise that it should never be allowed in the front room and should be locked away whenever Gloria was loose.

Bridget, I called it, after a young woman who had lately clawed my heart, and as long as I fed her regularly and treated her as a superior being we got on happily together. She was always on the look-out for a dab at Gloria, and I had to be pretty sharp sometimes to keep her out of the canary's room.

I grew fat with food and content at Mrs Murphy's, and it was a nasty shock when I came home one wet evening to find my suitcase packed and standing on the doorstep, the sound of female sobbing coming from the window and Mr Murphy waiting in the doorway. He handed me my mackintosh and a brown-paper parcel of my books.

"What's up, Mr Murphy?" I asked. "Why all this?"

He took his pipe out of his mouth and pointed it at my chest.

"Out," he said. "Your cat ate 'er bird."

And he closed the door.

37

I stood there in wonder, stunned, not by the shock of eviction but by the marvellous economy of his words, the perfection of his narrative, the stark, crystal precision of his style. Every detail of the melancholy tragedy . . . three characters, two animals, death, violence, and retribution, were clear and condensed in those six little words.

I repeated them in admiration, standing there in the rain, in the evening, in the Old Kent Road.

"Out. Your cat ate 'er bird."

Dickens had handled it and we'd have been into the third chapter before the birdcage dealer got off the stagecoach; Proust, and four volumes would be gone before the idea of a canary became concrete in Mrs Murphy's mind; ten pages of Joyce and we'd all still have been praying in the public bar—but for Mr Murphy six words sufficed, six words of one syllable, nineteen letters, leaving out the aitch. And even Hemingway kept in the aitches.

I picked up my case and went out to find a new home. Tossed out again, but this time the lesson was worth it. I had beheld perfection and was satisfied. I savoured the line aloud again.

"Out. Your cat ate 'er bird."

A passing policeman looked at me hopefully as I trudged through the rain. One day, I said to myself —one day, Mr Murphy . . .

PATRICK RYAN

Literary Zodiac

'Behind the man the writer moles away.'
                    The Sunday Times on H. E. Bates.

THE writer tenebrously moles away;
He beavers at his manuscript all day;
Occasionally he'll sloth awhile and brood
Before (or after) pythoning some food.
His publisher gorillas when he's heard
The author tortoises from word to word;
The agent squirrels at the long delay.
While the tax-gatherer spiders for his prey.

R. A. PIDDINGTON

Dig that Crazy Bed

WITH many others, no doubt, I was interested by a recent gardening piece in *The Observer* recommending the rhubarb-lover to feed this December-planted beauty on an old flock mattress. "Dig it in," wrote Mr L. D. Hills, "at the rate of about a barrow-load to four square yards . . . buy one from a second-hand furniture shop . . . Confirm that it is not cotton but wool, a slow-acting organic nitrogen manure that needs supplementing with a pound of bonemeal to that area for immediate rhubarb requirements." I quote at length in case anyone thinks I am making this up.

Frankly, though, I am not feeding my rhubarb on mattresses this year. I've tried for two years without making a real success of it. In December, 1956, I didn't even get the mattress out of the shop, owing to the unco-operativeness of the proprietor, a Mr Bidging, of Southwark. He was a man of some individuality, and got the idea that I was trying to make a fool of him.

"What size bed?" he asked, going to the back of the shop and stirring a pile of mattresses with his foot.

"I'm not sure," I said. "I should think about ten feet by twelve."

He said he'd never heard of a bed that size.

"It's a rhubarb bed," I told him, and he came back and leant on the counter, and said that the date was December 17, not April 1, and he'd got a busy morning, with three second-hand dressing-tables to deliver at Loughton, Essex. He said he hadn't got a mattress ten feet by twelve, and no pigeon's milk either.

It took me a minute or two to calm him down.

When I said I'd settle for an ordinary double-bed size he pulled one out and brought it. He said he had the same thing in blue. I said the colour didn't matter, because it would have earth all over it.

"Earth?" he said.

"Never mind—I'm sorry I mentioned it. Tell me," I said, "how many barrow-loads of stuff do you suppose there is here?"

He said he'd never sold mattresses by the barrow-load. He tried to take it away again, but I hung on to my end. I said I'd take it, provided he'd confirm that it was filled with slow-acting organic nitrogen manure, and he wrenched it out of my hands, splitting two finger-nails (mine—I didn't ask about his) and went to the back of the shop and telephoned the police.

That was 1956. But last year, when I'd got up enough nerve to tackle the problem again, I went to a local man, and adopted a more flat-footed approach. I told him the whole plot from the start, and apart from asking for the money before I took the mattress out to the car, he behaved very reasonably. I drove home in high spirits, under the impression that my troubles were over. At that time, of course, I had not considered the technique of actually digging a mattress into clay soil at the rate of about a barrowload to four square yards.

For those who plan to do this as a result of Mr Hills' article I would recommend, first, a particularly sharp spade and teeth not in need of dentistry. Not that the teeth are actually employed in tearing the ticking. But the sensation of driving even a sharp spade into a strongly-finished flock mattress sets them on edge. Anyone who has bitten a tennis-ball

will understand my meaning. Secondly, ensure a clear operating area of at least twice the size of the bed; the rhubarb-bed, that is. Once the mattress is breached the contents tend to flow freely, as with fire-fighting foam, and can cover an average back-garden in no time, including climbing the summer-house steps and engulfing the garden-rollers, heaps of peat covered with tarpaulins, etc., in no time. The task of controlling the moving, creeping mass is especially difficult for hay-fever addicts or sufferers from kindred diseases, as continuous sneezing may set in, eyes stream, and feet itch unbearably as the penetrating fragments creep over wellington tops. In addition, wives and neighbours may panic and summon various emergency services whose presence merely adds to the confusion.

In my own experiment of last year any idea of ultimate rhubarb had gone with the wind after the first five minutes, and my only concern was to recapture the monster I had loosed. In the end, and with the assistance of a strong laundryman and two youths who had come to deliver the paraffin, we succeeded in throwing up rectangular earthworks and containing the enemy. The providential paraffin was then poured over it and the whole set alight. It burned for three days, and my wife and I took turns to sit up with it at night. A curious circumstance was that the night sky was filled with springs. These had been firmly gripped by flock until the flames did their work, but were then released in rather picturesque red-gold showers, some falling, with a dramatic hiss, as far away as the lily-pond of our next door neighbour but one.

I have not yet decided whether to try again next year. This year we are still looking for something that will grow on nine inches of charcoal with a light sprung-steel dressing.

J. B. BOOTHROYD

*　　　*　　　*

"The Duke of Norfolk . . . has earned a new honour. He has been appointed an admiral—of the Sussex Yacht Club. . . . The position is purely honorary—there is not even a uniform—and the duke will have no particular duties to perform. . . . Says the club president . . . 'Of course, he could preside over our regattas if he were present. But I do not really expect him to attend'. . . . The Duke, fifty, is tireless in the performance of public duties. . . ."

Sunday Express

No wonder.

Growing Familiar

My baby knew me as a face
Suspended over her in space.

My toddler knew me to the knees
As nylon eights and court-shoe threes.

My child of half a dozen Springs
Best knew me by my apron-strings.

Now that our sizes are the same
She knows me by my Christian name.

HAZEL TOWNSON

For Tiny Tots

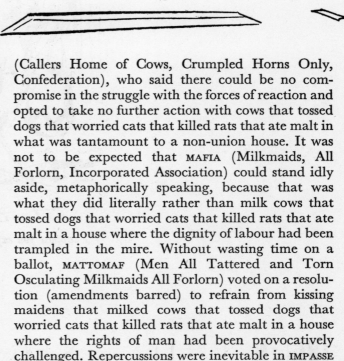

All characters are fictitious and bear no resemblance to any living trade unionists such as London dockers who struck unofficially to cut off the supply of imported meat in support of Smithfield drivers who struck for a 15 per cent wage increase because the speed limit for heavy vehicles was raised from 20 to 30 m.p.h.

THE House that Jack built was almost finished when a plastic pentagonal hod was introduced enabling an extra half-brick to be carried without adding to the total weight. This led to a strike by JOB (Jacobean Operative Builders). Already there lay in the basement a first consignment of malt, Jack being a spare-time brewer when not oppressing the workers, so a gesture of solidarity was demanded from MAUMAU (Maltsters and Unfederated Maltsters Associated Union), who refused to touch malt lying in a "hot" house. This touched off ROW (Rodent Operative Workers) who decided on a show of hands, some rather badly bitten, to decline to catch rats that ate malt in a house where trade union principles had been flagrantly violated. Practical sympathy was voiced by SCALP (Society of Catsmeat and Liver Purveyors), who denied service to cats that killed rats that ate malt in a house where democracy was being spat upon as though it were a Jewish gabardine. Whereupon DOGMA (Dog-collar Makers Association) were hurriedly convened under an emergency regulation and ceased upon the midnight hour to make collars for dogs that worried cats that killed rats that ate malt in a house where naked exploitation was unbridled, nay, rampant.

In a trice the fat was in the fire with CHOCCHOG

(Callers Home of Cows, Crumpled Horns Only, Confederation), who said there could be no compromise in the struggle with the forces of reaction and opted to take no further action with cows that tossed dogs that worried cats that killed rats that ate malt in what was tantamount to a non-union house. It was not to be expected that MAFIA (Milkmaids, All Forlorn, Incorporated Association) could stand idly aside, metaphorically speaking, because that was what they did literally rather than milk cows that tossed dogs that worried cats that killed rats that ate malt in a house where the dignity of labour had been trampled in the mire. Without wasting time on a ballot, MATTOMAF (Men All Tattered and Torn Osculating Milkmaids All Forlorn) voted on a resolution (amendments barred) to refrain from kissing maidens that milked cows that tossed dogs that worried cats that killed rats that ate malt in a house where the rights of man had been provocatively challenged. Repercussions were inevitable in IMPASSE (Incumbents, Marrying Priests, All Shaven and Shorn, Executive). Though this was a secular matter a dispensation was obtained to relieve them from the office of marrying men that kissed maidens that milked cows that tossed dogs that worried cats that killed rats that ate malt in a house where the Tolpuddle Martyrs lived again.

The ultimate action came from SOBSTUFF (Sellers of Bird Seed to Universal Feathered Friends). Could they support aggressive cocks that crowed in the morn that waked the priests that married men that kissed maidens that milked cows that tossed dogs that worried cats that killed rats that ate malt in a house where the memory of Keir Hardie was being mocked? No, at least not until strike funds ran out when all the unions had lent each other all their money as a gesture of solidarity.

LESLIE MARSH

41

Anton
The Female Species

'I suppose you expect a tip?'

'Madam is not at home, nor am I.'

'If I remember rightly, you never asked us to your table.'

'You go first, I'm frightened.'

'Are you seriously asking this court to believe that although you were standing right at the scene you didn't see a thing?'

43

Science Specialist

I SPENT two years in the Science Sixth doing A-level G.C.E.
And three more reading Physics and Maths. for my B.Sc. degree,
But by then I was tired of the world of Things with all its pumps and sanities
And I thought for a change I would bask a while in the warmth of the Humanities.
So I made myself known to an angry young man who spoke after lunch at the Rotary
Who got me into the inner set of a long-haired duffel-coterie.

It was only then that I understood what being in a groove meant,
For the poets I met were immobilized in something called 'The Movement,'
And they promptly complained of feeling sick when I ventured to quote a canto
Of the O-level stuff I had done at school, like *Drake's Drum* and *Lepanto*.
When I mentioned my favourite authors, too, they gave a derisive hoot,
Though my list began with Ray Bradbury and included Nevil Shute.

Now, I like a good book and I like a good play but I flatly refuse to grovel
Before pundits who pontificate on The Drama and The Novel,
So I'm back at my bench and my solenoids where at least I shan't be attacked
By a critic more carping than Nature, or one more unfeeling than Fact;
For we men of Science are sensitive souls and averse to causing pain,
But the experts in the Humanities are damn well inhumane.

E. V. MILNER

In the Country

successive crops from ground which had not been cultivated for three years previously, would be regarded as the owner of that ground". Naturally then, landlords saw to it that they cultivated every bit they could.

Perhaps we need similar legislation, for as you travel in an English train you can see acres and acres of land growing nothing—but pipe dreams for commuters.

RONALD DUNCAN

In the City

A FRIEND of mine who lived in St James and worked in Piccadilly used to reach his office by walking down Pall Mall, up Lower Regent Street, then along Jermyn Street. He made this unnecessarily long detour every day. When I once asked him why he did not take the short cut through the Green Park, he replied that he preferred his accustomed route because he "could not bear the sight of the country at any price".

But he was an exception. From my observation, it appears that the majority of Londoners are frustrated countrymen. As you walk down any street, you will see signs of this: pathetic little basement gardens, window boxes, rabbits in hutches, hens in yards. Luxury flat décor is now made up of trailing vines, rubber plants and fernery to camouflage the urban background.

On the other hand, I have had several farm-workers leave my employ this year for no other reason than that they were bored with the country. The drift to the towns is now a flood. It would seem that people want it both ways. The fortnight's holiday a year doesn't satisfy the townsman; the occasional day in the city isn't enough of the fleshpots for the countryman.

In America some attempt to solve this problem has been made where half a dozen city families join together to buy a farm. A permanent bailiff is employed by them collectively; and they take it in turn to spend a month on the farm. No doubt such a scheme lends itself to much squabbling. Community living is essentially an idea which works only over a coffee table in Gower Street.

But it does seem ridiculous that we should have several million frustrated countrymen and, at the same time, several million derelict acres, and can find no way of introducing one to the other.

In China a law was made five thousand years ago which stated that "any person who could take three

ONE of the features of the march of economic civilization is the increasing proportion of man's energies and ingenuity devoted to the entertainment of his fellow men. Mechanization and automation are pushing in the same direction. As fewer workers are needed for the basic pursuits such as the production of food, coal, steel, engines and the rest, more will be available to satisfy the less essential needs. It was pointed out recently that in the United States more than 60 per cent of the working population is now engaged in providing services such as retail selling, entertainment, beautifying, etc., and less than 40 per cent in actually making things. If this be the trend, then it follows that the greatest scope for expansion in business and profits lies with industries that cater for the pleasures rather than the basic needs of mankind.

Translated in more specific terms, this principle is well illustrated by one of the most spectacular of all the little boomlets that have recently been found in British industry, namely, in the sale of gramophone records and of the hi-fi reproducers that go with it.

It was once assumed that with the advent of sound broadcasting and later of television the gramophone would vanish. Far from it; the sale of records in Great Britain, which totalled £5,000,000 in 1947, had doubled in 1953, had doubled again in 1957, and is expected to reach between £22,000,000 and £23,000,000 this year. The record companies have been making good profits. Electric and Musical

Industries and Decca are reputed between them to manufacture 75 per cent of the records sold in this country. Each has interests spread well beyond the manufacture of records. They produce radio and television sets. They have also dug deeply into the electronics field which with its industrial applications comes into the sphere of automation.

And so we come round full circle. These two companies, and there are some others besides them, help to create the vacuum of leisure by making the machines that do man's work and even some of his thinking, and then they proceed to fill that vacuum with their radio and television sets, gramophones and long-playing records. It is a perfect formula.

LOMBARD LANE

To the Chairman of the Smithfield Meat Inquiry

Sir,—I am sorry I was unable to attend on the second day of your inquiry to give evidence re a forequarter that came in half (making two fore-eighths as we say) due to the delivery man absent-mindedly handling one end of it to a humper and the other end to a bummaree while his attention was distracted by an altercation between the scalesman and the cutter over some kidneys believed to have been improperly handled by one of the night men, but the fact is I came over very queer just after reading the first day's evidence in a piece of newspaper my tearer-upper happened to be handing to my wrapperee for a couple of chops I'd just sold to a member, if you'll forgive the expression, of the general public, and the long and short of it was I was taken off to hospital for checking.

Well, sir, it's no business of mine but if you could have seen the way I was handled you would know where to hold your next inquiry. No discourtesy, mind, but the lack of organization! Everybody doing half a dozen jobs, and no proper scheme of distribution. Right at the start, when they were getting me out of the ambulance on a stretcher, I saw how it was going to be. "Whoa up there!" I said to the pullers-back. "Not beyond the tail-board, now."

I might as well have been talking to a haunch of mutton. Do you know, sir, the same pair of pullers-back (and one of them was the driver, if you ask me) not only pitched me right to the hospital door, they humped me clean through into Reception, and not a word said by anyone or a blow struck in anger. I didn't know where to look, I felt so ashamed to see two pairs of hands doing the work of six.

It's the same all along in these places. Take the night women, for a start. I stood it as long as I could, being a stranger in the place if you follow my meaning, but when I saw the same girl bring my breakfast down the ward I made up my mind to speak out.

"What's wrong, then?" I asked her. "Where's the traymen this morning?"

"Traymen?" she said.

"The food humpers," I said. "Breakfasteers. Kedgerees. *I* don't know what you call 'em here. The point is, what are you thinking of, handling food?"

She said the night nurses always brought the breakfast round.

Of course I did my best to explain it to her. "Where's your pride in your job?" I said. "Bringing round hot-water bottles, tucking in sheets, handing out aspirins, humping porridge—this that and the other all night long, it's a proper muddle. *And* it was you took my temperature round about the time the market opens, unless I'm much mistaken."

She said it was.

"That's skilled work, that is," I told her. "You stick to that and let others do the casual jobs. Licensed men and such. You'll never get the rate for the job if you don't specialize. Look at your own surgeons," I said. "You won't catch a lung man working on a knee joint, now will you?"

She said to lie quiet and not worry. Well!

They had my appendix out in the finish, and a nasty shock I had on the way to the cutter, let me tell you. It was while I was talking to the wheeler-in, just to make conversation as you might say, and I happened to ask what she reckoned to pull in in a good week. Well, she hummed and hawed and came over a bit mind-your-own-business, but in the end she let drop that she was on some kind of weekly wage.

"My God!" I said. "Where's the incentive? Don't you realize that licensed bummarees get one-and-three a hindquarter? Four times that is five bob per patient, less perhaps ten per cent for live meat being easier to handle, and there you are with four-and-six a time for wheeling in, plus a bit under that for wheeling out according to what the cutter has been up to. *And* as many as you like on one trolley," I said, "with no reduction for quantity. If they want good keen work, they've got to pay for it," I told her.

"Look," I said. "If you don't want to tell me what you get p.w., all right. Say £20. Say £30. My point is you get the same however many you wheel along. So you take your time, see? Well, look at us now, just ambling down the corridor. Put you on piece-work, and you'd soon see the difference. You'd have twice as many through the theatre and done with in the time," I said.

"Don't tell me you've not got twice as many to

put through," I interrupted her, when she started to argue. "I know all about your waiting lists. A fine scandal there'd be if we had a tenth as much held up in store as what you've got in your line of business. It's organization and efficiency and every man to his job *and* a proper rate for it that's wanted here," I told her.

Well, then she got properly angry, sir, and came out with a lot of hot air I took no notice of, only in the middle of it she let slip her salary, and a real jolt it gave me.

"Hey!" I said. "Hold on," and I did a bit of calculating. "You mean to say you get less for humping me into this theatre—*me*," I said, "with four branches in south-east London—than if I'd been an aitchbone," I said, "or a forequarter of lamb?"

She hadn't looked at it like that, she said, and pretty soon after that they gave me a jab in the arm and I lost the thread of the argument. But I dare say I've told enough of what goes on here to let you and your colleagues understand you are wasting your time over this little business of bummarees being otherwise engaged, and the sooner you get round to these hospital places the better.

It's no business of mine, as I say, but if you ask me I'd sum up what's wrong under five main heads:

> *Slow throughput*
> *Low rates of pay*
> *Lack of specialization among nurses*
> *Unrestricted practices*

and, worst of all of course, old-fashioned methods of handling. Why, do you know sir, that when I was ready for collection, instead of having a delivery man hand me over to a licensed porter in the proper way, they let my wife put my hat on and hump me home in our bubble-car? Look at the waste of money somebody might have earned!

H. F. ELLIS

President de Gaulle

I⊤ is said of President de Gaulle
That the iron has entered his soul;
Pig-iron, one assumes it to be,
In a man as obstinate as he.

NICOLAS BENTLEY

The Music Goes Round and Round

Ruminations on the finals of the National Brass Band Championship of Great Britain at the Royal Albert Hall. FANCIERS and supporters, small men with new trilby hats and upturned overcoat collars, have breakfasted in Corner Houses on sausages and canned beans. They now roll up in shared taxi-cabs, five a time. Their chins are blue. They suck at cigarette stubs held inside bunched fingers. Some are rippers and shot-firers on perpetual night-shift a mile underground. To these the mists, smells and vistas of Kensington Gore at nine-thirty of an October morning must be disturbingly unreal.

Bandsmen clomp out of motor-coaches, stretch their legs, rebutton their frogged tunics. Euphoniums jacketed in leather are unshipped from enormous boots. ("Eighty-one competing bands; two thousand players; nine tons of instruments worth £200,000," exults a hand-out.) From humming green vans cables snake into the Albert Hall, a sign that what they call (why, I wonder?) the brass band 'movement,' a humble, horny-handed thing aesthetically considered has been taken up for petting and patting by the B.B.C.'s top culture boys.

May not this culture thing be something of a blight? Ears that crave for John Philip Sousa and his like are sentenced to chain performances of a test piece knocked together for the occasion by some hale and honoured English composer who privately thinks the brass band movement a bore but is gallantly prepared to make a democratic go of it. The piece he turns in is full of neo-Tudor jollities that make the heart sink. Lots of clever solo bits. Under a roof as far off as a sky lone cornets send up girlish notes. A ruminant B flat baritone moos uncertainly. Considered as a piece of carpentry or crochet work, the fugal finale is splendid.

Between breakfast time and tea (there is no lunch break) twenty-one bands, finalists all, troop on and off the platform. By noon the hall is jammed and hot. Everybody chain-smokes. Officials mop foreheads; even the shot-firers take off their overcoats, or at least turn down their collars. In rich blue fug the chrysanthemum baskets seem to float unsuspended over the platform. In its high niche the spot-lit championship vase ("Solid silver—takes two men to lift it," whispers a steward) glitters ethereally; the fug has turned it into a wraith.

A retired major comes on with the Cromarty Ketchup Band and conducts it with unleashed passion. When the music is sinister he takes two backward paces and crouches demonically. When the music is pretty he rises on his toes, throws his head back ecstatically and turns it sideways, as if he can't stand the sight of his players. He sweats liberally in all moods. The Ketchup flügelhorn solo gets mutual winks of approval from the old hands. Rosy K., the flügelhorn in question, has a chestnut perm, epaulettes of gold cord and a maroon tunic miles too big for her, because the one she ordered from the tailor didn't turn up on time and she had to borrow the fourteen-stone drummer's.

Nodding at her rucked sleeves her husband says playfully, "You're taking up the concertina, I see." The husband, foreman in the vinegar, is Ketchup's second cornet. He has a "cold spot" on his upper lip directly under his left eye, so is playing today on the other side of his mouth. This gives his performance a confidential look.

In one of the far, bleak oubliettes where bands titivate themselves and line up for the platform, press photographers take pictures of Rosy kneeling with her flügelhorn in front of a wall mirror. A man goes

'Sit!'

49

round shouting for mutes and collects them in a cardboard box. Somebody offers five-to-one on the Shotfirers' Benevolent and Philanthropic and is taken by a cheer-leader for Plastic Rocking Horses Welfare Silver.

First prize of 200 guineas and the championship challenge trophy has been won with 193 marks by Cromarty Ketchup. Up come the Ketchup players to be invested on the platform, by sergeant commissionaires, with gold-fringed sashes of honour.

Since morning three judges have been listening unseen in a white box uncommonly like a cold store. Stunned and groping they now make their way on to the platform. One is a mild composer with white hair and gold-rimmed spectacles who staggered himself at sixty by writing a royalty-milking ballad about

aching hearts. Another is a saturnine counterpoint professor who clicks his double-jointed fingers like castanets. The third is musical director of a Guards

regiment. While in the cold store he changed from mufti into major's uniform. His salute gets a flattered hand.

Then the awards.

Plastic Rocking Horses Welfare Silver are down the drain. Shot-firers' Benevolent and Philanthropic bite the dust. In the Tube, on their way to Corner House high teas, the vanquished exchange dry sentiments about conductors who aren't what they're cracked up to be, judges who don't wash their ears, band secretaries who mess up rehearsal dates, lose band parts, tread on clarinets and move useless resolutions about false teeth and compulsory retirement at eighty-five.

"Still, Harry, let's be fair. Ketchup aren't that bad."

"They'll do."

CHARLES REID

Floreat Ministerium !

A peep into the day when the Victory for Socialism group have fulfilled their plan to take over the public schools.

SO you're at Eton, are you, comrade, heh-heh?

Why do you say "comrade" in that extraordinary way?

Well, it must be a bit different there since the Labour Government took it over, I imagine.

Oh, I suppose it is. Thank God I didn't know what it was like before.

But surely——

Of course it may not have been as bad as it sounds, but it must have been a bit off when anyone who had enough money could send their children there just by putting their names down. And those terrible little cads they used to send as guinea-pigs at one period, with no proper people and a tendency to eat curry with a knife and fork. I can't imagine how ghastly it was.

There weren't many guinea-pigs, as you call them.

I didn't call them, it was Warren Chetham-Strode. Anyway, it's perfectly all right now, because Stephen Swingler's made it impossible for anyone to get in unless he's a decent fellow. Actually, what he said was that boarding schools were to be provided for children who needed them on social or emotional grounds. I don't know how many of the fellows here actually claim to have got into Eton on emotional grounds, unless it means that they made a frightful stink when they were told they'd been put down for Harrow or Winchester or somewhere; but I do know that on social grounds most of them need it very much.

But if the Ministry of Education said they were to go to Harrow, how could they get it changed so that they went to Eton?

Well, Stephen Swingler arranged for that. He said parents should be allowed freedom of choice where the freedom is important, and going to Eton is important, I should have said, wouldn't you?

But he also said that it shouldn't be allowed where the acquisition of arbitrary privilege was the object of the choice.

I can't imagine what he meant by arbitrary privilege, but whatever it is you don't get any of it at Eton. It's different at Winchester, where I believe you get colours for politics.

Aren't you exaggerating a bit?

Well, how do you explain Dick Crossman, and Douglas Jay, and Hugh Gaitskell, and Stephen Swingler——

Come now, you must get your facts right. Mr Swingler was at Stowe.

What's Stowe?

It's a school. A public school.

Well, it only goes to show how under-privileged I am not to know all these things. Anyway, things are a jolly sight better at Eton since it's been administered by the Ministry of Education.

How, for instance?

It's more democratic, for one thing. At m'shop steward's——

I beg your pardon?

It would have been "m'tutor's" in your time, I suppose. Anyway, m'shop steward leaves quite a lot of discipline to the Library, which is a sort of National Executive of the boys. Well, not a National Executive, really; that would be Pop.

Good heavens, you don't really mean that you still have Pop?

Did *you* have it? I didn't know Eton was so democratic in your day.

But surely democracy is just what Pop doesn't stand for. Surely Pop stands for arbitrary privilege if anything does.

It stands for Popular Overseers' Presidium, actually. I thought it was one of the things Stephen Swingler brought in. Most of the good things are. I believe before the Government took it over the place was terribly uncomfortable—a little room you'd hardly put a housemaid in at home, and the bath-water always tepid, and so on.

And it's better now?

Oh, it really isn't at all bad now. You see, what happened after the Swingler Act was first passed was that a whole lot of sort of working-class boys turned up before they discovered that they weren't really suited to it on emotional grounds, and they took one look at the place and hurtled back to their sordid little homes on the next bus. So they had to make it at least tolerably comfortable, and make the food a bit less poisonous, so that these funny little numbers could be persuaded to stay. Not that they were persuaded, actually, after it was explained to them that they could only see their mums during the holidays and at Long Leave; but they had to try.

I see. But it must have put the fees up enormously.

Oh, there aren't any fees. After the Swingler Act all the endowments of all the public schools were sort of vested in either the Ministry of Education or the Charity Commissioners for the benefit of education generally, sort of, and Eton was really quite well endowed and it costs rather a lot to run, so they just earmarked its endowments and used them for the college. And of course it gets all the usual grants that go to State Schools, whatever they are—I'm a bit vague about it. But I know we do all right. I believe the Director-General actually got a rise.

Who's that?

The Provost, I think he used to be called.

I don't believe I'd know the place if I went back.

Oh, but you'd like it. It's terribly enlightened and democratic. There's a frightfully good system we have called fagging.

But——

It's based on the old apprenticeship system, you see. A boy is attached to an older boy and does odd jobs for him and so on while he's learning. M'shop steward says it's an ideal blend between the contemporary and the traditional.

And what do you suppose Mr Swingler thinks of all these reforms of his?

Oh, I should think he'd be enormously pleased, wouldn't you? It's all worked out so well, hasn't it?

B. A. YOUNG

52

Just a Minute, Matron

SPEAKING as a man who, so far and touch wood, has spent very little of his life in hospital—either as a patient or a visitor—I find myself heartily in disagreement with Miss Powell, the matron of St George's Hospital.

Miss Powell, I need not remind you, said the other day that the waking of patients at five o'clock "is a pernicious practice," and I should like to know what Miss Powell proposes to do about it. Has she considered the patients' own feelings in the matter? What changes has she in mind? Does she realize that out-patients like me are violently opposed to the mollycoddling of in-patients, to any moves that would make the word hospitalization more attractive?

I usually awake at six-fifteen. In agony. The pain produced by a small boy bouncing on the abdomen can be excruciating. There is a moment of unbelieving panic, a bewildering return of consciousness, and then the stark reality of another day. And small boys do not always land on the abdomen: they sometimes get across the main aorta or drive a knee of iron into an exposed ear. Given a choice between a nurse's sponge and a small boy's mass I know what my decision would be.

I never have time, on being rudely awakened, to reflect on the joys of *le five o'clock* at St George's or other hospitals. A patient returns to life gradually. The ward lights are switched on, bathing his eyelids in the rosy artificial glow of dawn. There are exciting noises off—the rustle of a starched apron, the bell-like chime of enamel and clinical porcelain. And there by his side stands Miss Nightingale ready to assure him that he is looking better, that his temperature and pulse are normal and that it is raining.

Raining. The patient can now occupy his mind with beautiful thoughts.

1) Only an hour to go, and with a little bit of luck there will be a cup of tea. (Thank you, night nurse.)

2) Only two hours to breakfast.

3) Only three hours before the arrival of the man with the morning papers.

4) Only five hours and that nice house doctor will be on his rounds.

The mind refuses to be cabined by the hospital. Think of all those poor fools, those idiotic out-patients who are still asleep! Wasting the best years of their lives. Don't they realize that the great thinkers and writers have always done their best work before breakfast? Balzac was up at five, scribbling like mad. Arnold Bennett already had a chapter or two under his belt before the corn-flakes arrived.

Another hour or two and all those silly old bread-winning out-patients will be struggling into bathrooms and cold kitchens, scraping at chins and pieces of toast, swallowing deplorable coffee and chunky headlined news, dashing for the bus or train . . . and rubbing their tired eyes. The dopes! And it is raining.

How much better to awaken early, mother dear, and be truly alive at five.

Of course not all out-patients are stirred from slumber by the ebullient gymnastics of small boys. There are also small girls. There are also:

(*a*) aircraft flying too low and much too near one's chimneys

(*b*) lorries carrying cans full of hammers and lead shot

(*c*) milkmen

(*d*) birds with little concrete-mixers caught in their throats

(*e*) more milkmen

(*f*) dogs, cats, poultry

(*g*) clogs (a regional touch)

(*h*) shunting engines

(*i*) burned toast (*is* there anything more deafening than the din of heavily scorched sliced bread being abraded with a blunt kitchen knife?)

(*j*) whistling newspaper boys

(*k*) wives.

Miss Powell should think less of her pampered inmates, more of the world's long-suffering out-patients. After all, it is from us that she must in the long run draw her clients.

BERNARD HOLLOWOOD

'*No thanks—I'm trying to give it up.*'

Night of The Short Thoughts

THE Renaissance is down if not out. The written word as the prime tool of mental training shuffles to the exit like a slapped clown. The well-nourished, wide-ranging, literary mind is being told to take the earth seriously and to concentrate on one of the myriad banalities that make up physical science. Heat warms, ice cools, cars stall, things fall, light bends, motion ends. The passionate convolutions of poetry and art are to be pushed back out of the arena to make way for these clownish simplicities. The ancient educational aim of making a man's mind, through verbal communication only, a self-contained and instantly available theatre of dignity and grace has gone by the board.

We may not in future produce an Aristophanes, a Shakespeare or a Keats. But we shall without question produce with our own elfin hands a thunderstorm, an earthquake and a few Peloponnesians with stiff collars and a wonder cure for the phthisis which they didn't have when we got around to them in the first place. The edict has gone forth against cerebration in loneliness and for its own sweet sake. The educable young are now directed to the dour team-work of acolytes all involved in some crass bit of conjuring to sharpen the tempo of death, transport or digestion.

The life of the intelligent, from the fifteenth century onwards, was cheap and exciting. Given quietness, a few companions and access to a few books that have dealt on a level above the probation officer's with the rhythm of man's anguish and joy, you had the makings of a university of exhilaration.

Ever since the end of the Middle Ages when the priest, the peasant and the artisan imposed their own curious limitations on the scope of thought and discussion, the witless, those malevolent and so dangerous ones, the unimaginative and pompous, have been planning their own peculiar Night of the Short Thoughts. True, they have had their moments of imbecile intransigence when the fanatically literate, who hold the wall against the gutterine hordes who yearn for the womb-like peace of an unschooled world, have for a moment dozed. Their dream has ever been to banish the pain of difficult thought, the most terrible rod an evolving species can make for its own bare back.

Now their hopes are rising, as the Classics and the Humanities rush to their eclipse. A fistful of digital expertise is now to be worth a headful of imaginative brilliance. Under cover of those prim experimenters to whom the laboratory is the Ark of the Covenant, the proponents of an aseptic coolness for a species whose trade mark is an untidy heat, the turnip-heads will advance to power. The poet will perish on a pyre of bunsen burners tended by a world full of glassy-eyed intellectual vestals, virgin of any of the authentic raptures that first planted warmth in the entrails of our tribe.

The men who are directing the present educational swing in favour of scientific teaching are still sophisticates in the old university tradition, fluently ambivalent in their cultural loyalties. But wait until the morons take over, the uninhibited bustlers who would trade Verdi's *Requiem* and *King Lear* for one well-washed retort.

In the meantime the schools rush to meet their darkish and rather shabby destiny. The amount of boiling, measuring, counting, mixing rises daily. Books are pushed into far corners to make way for the running tide of fetid pipettes. The Science VIth is now a procession of white-coated votaries. The Arts VIth, the few beagles who are still panting in the wake of man's history and his spirit's expression, is in full retreat. Those who turn away giddy from this whirling jig of weighing and probing will meet as a kind of Mafia by moonlight to swap a line of Rilke for an aphorism of Gide before going to immolate themselves on the electrified fences of the nearest Gamma-ville.

The industrial background of our ancestors had been long and consistent, from Bronze Age pixies to Steam Age colliers, and we were kept on a cunning tether. When our ideas became too arrogantly Platonic we could always be whipped back into the nearest foundry. It did not work in my case. I was an inept metal worker. I set the iron and allied trades farther back than they had ever been since things picked up at Jarrow. I got out from under just in time.

Does this mania to be excluded from the most potent contemporary cult rest on a genuine incapacity or a real philosophic revulsion? Do I think that the classical, book-centred, literary education was a kind of course in compassion that served to sweeten the human lump and that without it the thoughts of man about men will become more boorish and sinisterly loveless? I have, at odd midnight moments, tried to reform, have fought with passion to see the growing pantomime of laboratory antics as something other than noisome irrelevancies. I report little progress. Einstein I can take, for his sad humility brings him into the mainstream of reassurance. But my heart hits the floor at the sight and thought of the crew of bombardiers, star-splitters and tinkers he helped to beget.

I have a dream. It begins off-key and bitter. I see a river bank. It is quiet, it is cool, in contrast with the lunatic heat and din that most human activity now wears. To the river bank come a group of men, like Abelard and his friends, who on the banks of the Seine, in reed huts, drawn by some mysterious appetite for light from the corners of Europe, set up a great new university of "more human letters". I engage in a little catechism with every new arrival.

"You have looked deep down into the heart of nature?"

"Fifteen years with the Geophysical Junta. I have seen the heart."

"How is it?"

"Black, treacherous, and, oh God, so boring."

"Good. Do you feel any shudder of a wish to boil anything?"

"No. Coolness is king."

"Do you believe in splitting things?"

"No. I believe in a rough kind of integrity. If things don't naturally want to expose their middles,

leave them alone, I say. What if some supernaturally wise and eternal thing came along with an urge to split the human?"

"Good. To dissect anything?"

"No. As little as my wish to be dissected."

"Good. To perform acts of addition or subtraction?"

"No. For me, two and two can do anything they like, except breed."

GWYN THOMAS

'Why aren't you messing about?'

55

'*For once I've remembered the tin opener.*'

Lady Chatterley's Companion

GREAT as the pleasure of being a linguist must be, the pleasures of not being one are even greater. No polyglot, for example, could share my enjoyment at seeing a poster outside a Copenhagen cinema advertising a film called *Lady Chatterley's Elsker*. "Elsker" it seems to me, is a nice, crisp word to strike off the tongue. Quite obviously it has no romantic or sexual connotation. No tenderness there; it is a brisk, no-nonsense, co-educational sort of word.

"It looks like rain—think I'll take my elsker with me."

"Yippee! Elskers for breakfast!"

"No elskers, hawkers, or circulars."

"Pair of elskers for sale. Hardly used—owner going abroad. £100 o.n.o." Elsker is *that* sort of word.

The trouble is that I have never read the somewhat elusive book of the film, and so have no idea what accessories Lady C. may have gathered about her. But I picture her red-faced and tweedy, attending, say, the Badminton Horse Trials clad in a nice, long, wool-lined elsker (how they do keep the wind off, to be sure!) or trudging her native moors with the guns accompanied by a hamper full of elskers baked to a golden turn on the griddle in the Chatterley kitchens.

(Also obtainable at Fortnum's on Wednesdays to those producing a Wine and Food Society card.) At Ascot too an elsker sounds a practical note—no one has ever yet been struck by lightning when wearing one, and at Wimbledon they are marvellous for protecting the eyes from the glare of the sun. At the Chelsea Flower Show there is nothing like some old but well-fitting elskers to avoid foot-fatigue, and at the Academy Private View if there is one thing that could be said to make Art tolerable it is a couturier-designed elsker. Jennifer writes from Heathfield that surely she is old enough to have her own elsker by *now*, and young Julian prays that his mother will not let him down and arrive elskerless on the Fourth. (The new nylon ones are astonishingly resistant to cream and strawberry stains too.) And, of course, to be snapped by the *Tatler* photographer at a moment when one has temporarily discarded one's elsker is nothing short of social disaster.

The British aristocracy has had its ups and downs. It may, or may not, as Miss Mitford avers, have its loot stashed away. But properly equipped it is bound to survive. Or as we linguists say "Floreat Elsker!"

MONICA FURLONG

Hunter's Morn

I CAN'T say that I like the hunting of the hare better than that of the fox.

There was a day, many years ago down near Crewkerne in Somerset, when they dragged me out of bed to go beagling in the crisp morning air. It must have been early September, and the meet, for some sensible country reason, was at 6 a.m., or not much later. My employer (I was supposed to be coaching a boy for Common Entrance—almost the only vacation job known to undergraduates in those genteel days) felt certain that I should enjoy the chance of an early morning run, and I felt equally certain that he would despise me if I refused. So I went. People who regret the passing of their youth forget some of the things they had to do in order not to be despised.

Running through roots before breakfast is all right up to a carapace, making so loud a noise that it threatens at times to drown even the rumblings of an empty stomach, there may come one of those moments of self-doubt, common to all mortal flesh, when one pauses to ask what is the purpose of it all.

When one like would to pause, rather. Time and again on that bright far-off September day the idea of a rest occurred to me, but always my employer was at my elbow, running with the tireless intentness of the early forties. His wife, too, sped lightly beside him on an all but printless toe, asking no quarter; and as for the boy, whose weakness at algebra was my especial concern, he ran with a careless exuberance that might have been deliberately designed to humiliate me. In such company it was difficult for a young man of twenty to suggest a breather. Even when there was a check, and others of the field were content to slow down to a walk or even stand motionless awaiting the hounds' convenience, this terrible trio allowed me no respite. "We'd better cut across to the top of the rise," my employer would cry, "in case she breaks right-handed," or some such nonsense; and off we would go through the unendurable stubble, while the sweet September sky reeled before my glazing eyes.

The pride of youth is a terrible thing. I could not bring myself to say that I must stop or die. Instead, I had recourse at last to a subterfuge of a kind that I now look back on with shame. We were passing close to a little copse, a mere half-acre or less of trees and shrubby undergrowth, and I was perhaps a pace or so behind the dauntless three when desperation gave me the idea. "Catch you up," I called to them, trying hard to keep the sob out of my breath, and turned left-handed into the trees.

My employer's wife half turned her head and had got as far as "What's the mat——?" when some feeling of delicacy that lingered on in those days even among beagling women (and upon which I was relying) checked her utterance and bore her, Diana-like, away. I was alone.

But not yet invisible. With the last ounces of my failing strength I dragged myself farther into the copse, deep into its inmost heart where the bushes grew close and thick and a myriad spiders' webs gleamed and sparkled in the stray beams of autumn sunlight. There, on a couch of wet leaves and grasses, I threw myself down and let the world go by. The sounds of the hunt grew distant and I was content that it should be so. It would be the easiest thing, later on, to explain that I had tried a short cut to catch up and lost my way, I had no idea at all, for the first two or three minutes I lay there, that the hare they were hunting was within a yard of me.

Her great dark eye was the first thing I saw, when I opened my own, regarding me with a sort of passionless despair. She was very spent, poor thing. Her fur was streaked with sweat, and her flanks

heaved more violently and swiftly even than my own. She feared me, naturally, but she did not move. Pure exhaustion, and perhaps some sense of kinship with this other bedraggled creature that had crept in there to die, held her still. So we lay side by side beneath the bushes, fetching long shuddering breaths.

I wanted most desperately to be able to communicate. I wanted to tell her that we were in this thing together, that I meant her no harm, and that if we both lay close and kept quiet they would never find us. I had forgotten, until the yelp of a distant hound reminded me, that an invisible, inexorable thread was stretched, for all its loops and whorls and doublings-back, between my companion and the hunt. Another hound gave tongue, and another, nearer. The hare quivered and stirred. "Stay where you are, you fool!" I whispered. A lunatic plan came into my mind of taking off my jacket and enveloping her in it with a swift throw, like a retiarius with his net. I thought that perhaps her scent would fail where she had entered the copse and that to save her I had only to keep her pinned in our retreat. I don't know. I suppose, if she had stayed with me, the beagles would have found us

there together; and a devil of a lot of explaining I should have had to do when the field came up. "Why on earth didn't you holla when you found her?" they would have said, and my employer and his wife would have turned their backs on me as on a person totally unfitted to instruct their backward child. Obviously it was better, for me, that the hare should bolt; and it would be possible to argue that there was a certain nobility in my desire to save her even at the risk of my own exposure. But I cannot pretend that I weighed the matter up in this way at all. My response was purely instinctive. Here were we, crouched in the shadows, in a jam together; outside, in the bright sunlight, was this horrible hunt, intent to get us both on the run again. Keep still then, puss, and let us sweat it out together.

A hound bayed, if beagles go so deep, quite close. With a sudden sideways bound the hare eluded my despairing clutch and went off through the bushes like the wind. I heard a shout, a tumult of yelping, and then once more I was lying there, quite alone this time, while the noises of the hunt grew distant and faded over the hill. But now I was less content that it should be so. Of course it was a simple instinct of self-preservation that sent her bounding out into the open. But in youth one is more sentimental, more prone to the sin of anthropomorphism. The thought was insistent with me that possibly, just possibly, she had reckoned that of the two of us poor hunted creatures it was I who was the more spent and desperate, and so had deliberately sacrificed herself to draw them off me. After a while, I got up and brushed the leaves from my hair and went slowly back to where the car was parked.

I had no feelings then, and have none now, against hunting or those who hunt. But since that September day I have liked the hunting of the fox better than that of the hare.

H. F. ELLIS

'Oil your baggage, sir?'

'I beat him!'

GRAN THEATRE
PRESENTS
SALOME

AN ORIGINAL
PRODUCTION
AUTHENTIC
COSTUMES
OPENING NIGHT MAY 13

The Artificial Respiration Controversy

THIS issue, which has been vexed for some time now, really started in Remember of last year when a delegate to the T.U.C. conference remarked in an interview that he thought that Artificial Respiration. Little more was heard, apart from an official denial, and most people thought that a natural death; however, a week later, an official announcement was made, on behalf, that they considered that Artificial Respiration, but in much stronger terms than. The original delegate responsible resigned from, saying that misquotation.

A question was asked in the House, replying to which the Parliamentary Under said that he had given the matter due.

"Bearing in mind," he continued, "and despite, the government is obliged to refrain from on this matter. We prefer to keep an open."

At this stage, representatives of the Arts expressed their opinions regarding. The bone of their was that this was a non-political and from the artists the view, with certain specific, was that Æsthetic. Two critics differed, protesting passionately that Old.

The unions re-entered the battle. This was a social, affecting the welfare of every working, and in view of the ever-increasing cost, drastic action should be. The railway workers said that they thought that greyhounds and occasionally beer. There was an unofficial, inspired by subversive, and many rumours of corruption by undesirable.

Letters to the were numerous and I acknowledge for quoting from:

"DEAR OLD CODGERS, What is all this about that Artificial Respiration? Me and the Old, we have thought for many years that a day in Blackpool, that is what me and the Old, all these years. And what is O.K. for me and the Old, that should be O.K. for.

In any case, what right have they to get up on their hind? And who do they think they anyway, that's what me and the Old think."

In contrast to we have:

"DEAR SIR, This has gone too far. A sense of must surely, in face of these Forces of in our, corrupting the Youth of our green and pleasant, this precious, this.

We are, thanks be to, still able to hold aloft, in the face, and notwithstanding. We will fight them on."

Three or four after the beginning of, there was a plea for, in the leader column of one of our most cherished.

"We must blend the best of Tradition with what Modern Science and Technology have seen fit to. The Nation is on its. Are we to split the? This will surely put it on. Let no one.

Be sure, friends, that the Commonwealth will."

Despite these numerous and various, the rival factions came to, on a number of. The police were obliged to, though a Scotland Yard spokesman denied that force. He emphasized that only good-humoured persuasion in the best English.

It seemed, for a short, that simmering down. Then like a bolt from, came the dramatic, the infamous letter from beyond.

"Artificial Respiration is now an international. The Western powers, by their ruthless suppression of, have seriously undermined the peace and security of all. The people have been denied their fundamental human, the right of individual.

"We have intercontinental guided, and provocation of this, blatantly capitalistic in its, will not be. We do not want a Third World. Let Wisdom, if such there still, before it is too."

Panic followed on this side of the Iron. There were wholesale, and many were the investors on the Stock Exchange who, it was reliably reported that emigration, despite adverse conditions known o bet existing in. Plans were made for emergency, the Home Guard was, and so were hundreds of air-raid shelters.

In the nick, an element of sanity was restored by the Prime, in a speech which might well go down. He agreed that troubled waters, but insisted that the Ship of State could. This would, of course, involve far greater exploitation of the peaceful uses. He had, however, unlimited faith in, and co-existence must at all costs.

Since then, some people have stopped crying that Inevitable; certainly, we all hope that somehow.

ALAN PLATER

'You are twelve stone:
you will soon be thirteen stone.'

MAHOOD

'It hurts here and here, doctor.'

HEATH

SIR,

I would like to correct the caption to Mahoods' picture in your issue of August 13. What Napoleon said was not, "It hurts here and here, doctor". It was, "It *itches* here and here".

Napoleon's characteristic gait was due to the unfortunate circumstance that he was not only wounded in his campaigns but also picked up scabies, of which the doctors could not cure him. Scabies has a preferential localization under the girdle. This compelled Napoleon to keep his hands under his coat on the waist-line in readiness to strike.

Yours faithfully,

A. B. L. BEZNAK, M.D.
Professor of Physiology

University of Ottawa

61

'That's what comes of them insisting on a 40-hour week, and you insisting on a scheduled launching.'

Let There Be Resonance

THE fact that I have been frightened off public speaking for life involves little real hardship to the community. I like to think that better men may be able to improve their voice production by studying the very text-book* which has left me with stultification of the glottis.

Dimly, I always suspected that clavicular breathing was at the root of my breathlessness. I had never stopped to consider that my tendency towards pedantic delivery ("It-tah izz-u allemoast-eh impossibullu too eelustrrait-ah in-eh pr-r-r-int-eh thee r-r-ay-zzoolt-ah ovv-uh this-s-s forlt-ah") was caused by, among other things, the rebound of explosive consonants.

But where I really fell down was in not knowing how to harness my soft palate and sinuses in order to improve the resonance of my speech.

"Keep the soft palate well raised . . ." begins one instruction by Mr Johnson. Now I know what the soft palate is; it is "the upper portion of the mouth at the back". In my time I have probably raised and lowered it a good deal but I can no more raise it to order than I can wag my ears. Other people no doubt can perform both feats, and I envy them.

One effect of lowering the soft palate, it seems, is to force the sounds to proceed through the nose, which is *not* the way to achieve a pleasing nasal resonance. Says Mr Johnson: "The true ring of reverberation of vocal sounds IN the nasal cavities BEFORE they are projected through the mouth should be cultivated."

Yes, Mr Johnson, but *how?* I tried this sort of thing forty years ago when I had hopes of becoming a professional ventriloquist ("with the lips almost closed, contract the glottis and use only the tip of the tongue") and I got nowhere.

On sinuses Mr Johnson says: "These best contribute to a resonant voice by the thinking of the sounds first UPWARDS (to the headbones and the bones of the mask of the face) and then FORWARDS (into the audience) WITHOUT UNDUE STRAIN OR FORCE". Elsewhere he asserts that thinking the tone into position is something which can be developed and stabilized by practice.

I spent twenty minutes trying to think sounds in and out of my sinuses and it is allemoast-eh impossibullu to describe the resultant noises; they were not

* "Practical Speech Training" by Harry Johnson (*Jenkins*).

unlike those which a certain type of elderly scholar makes to himself all day in the British Museum Reading Room.

At this stage I realized I was trying to do advanced senior exercises before I had mastered the simpler ones. Back I went to page 11 and with "lips spread like a smile" and "tongue arched towards the roof of the mouth" I tried to make the sound "ee" as in "heed". All I achieved was "glug", as in comic strip. I was in the same state of helpless unhappiness as when I tried deliberately to swallow a pill without crunching it.

The more I studied this book the more I began to think about anti-aircraft predictors. During the war a theory was evolved that nursemaids and barmaids might be able to operate these instruments more efficiently if they knew that when they turned a hand-wheel they were rotating Range through Time (or perhaps it was Time through Height). Such instruction tended to induce a state half-way between awe and catalepsy and eventually the idea was abandoned. The minxes were told not to bother how the thing worked but just to turn the wheel smoothly, like Corporal Smith. That's how it is with me. Tell me what my larynx and pharynx are doing, or what they ought to be doing, and I am a complete write-off.

I do not wish to suggest that it is impossible to improve one's speech with the aid of a text-book. After all, thousands of bashful young men learn to waltz and fox-trot by taking correspondence courses. Mr Johnson may tell me that his book is primarily designed for use in conjunction with the speech-training classes of the London College of Music, but the blurb assures me that it is "ideally suited as a self-tutor," and that is how I have been trying to use it.

Not all the exercises in this book are as exacting as those I have mentioned. I can recite the alphabet two and a half times without distress on one breath; alternatively, I can repeat the 16 letters after Mr Johnson's name four times. When I say "The dew fell heavily on the mountain" no one thinks I am describing the misadventures of a Hebrew explorer (in any event one rarely finds Jews on mountains; they have more sense). And ever since I heard a Glasgow magistrate urge a witness to ar'i'ula'e more clearly I have been very careful how I said "pickle bottle" and "Metropole Gardens". But the only reason I can say these phrases is because nobody ever told me what to do with my tongue and palate in order to pronounce them.

One object of this book is to encourage the speaking of received English; that is, the sort of English that is acceptable to top people. I wonder whether the author has not missed an opportunity here. Recent broadcast programmes have emphasized that certain classes of top people, like head-office bank managers, bishops and senior Staff Officers, all have

their own variants of received English. Those who aspire to success in these fields know that they must speak in the same subtly off-beat accents as their masters, or perish.

Will Mr Johnson, in a later edition, tell them how to manipulate their palates, their sinuses and, if necessary, their ears in order to achieve their ambition? He may immobilize a few incompetents like myself, but thousands of ambitious men and women will be lastingly grateful to him.

E. S. TURNER

The West, Doggone It

APART from Robin Hood and Ivanhoe, it seems that there were no characters in the whole of our long island story capable of being woven into an exciting series for television. It is one of the drawbacks of being British. Read any history book and you'll see why our producers gave up in despair: nothing colourful ever happened here. A few of our people did happen to sail around the world and discover a few odd places; there was a spot of scrapping now and then, and some of the most glorious and dashing scenes in the whole tapestry of human endeavour were stitched and coloured here with the blood and guts of our rude forefathers; but apart from that, there wasn't really anything much.

Fortunately, however, a long time ago—oh, way back—there were places in the U.S.A. where material was being created night and day, without a pause, exactly suitable for series after series—enough stuff to keep our TV screens jumping until kingdom

come. It was in the days when women wore hobble-skirts and 1958 hair-styles; when every six-shooter carried two dozen cartridges, and something like a couple of million people were shot neatly off their horses by pagan aborigines with bows and arrows while moving out West to discover Beverly Hills. Every man over eleven could fire a bullet at least four times further than any gun manufacturer ever claimed was possible, with an accuracy that would make a Bisley champion look like a fool. Everybody who was shot died instantly, except heroes, who were hit carefully in the fleshy part of the arm and nursed back to health in five minutes by the application of a hot-water bandage. Heroes were clean-shaven and eight feet tall, and looked about as much like human beings as Hoot Gibson, whom you won't remember. Character men were allowed to wear period clothes. Villains always cheated at poker, and were the only people sensible enough to shoot an enemy when he wasn't expecting it. Saloon tarts were never known to pursue their occupation, presumably because they were too busy rushing about with all those hot-water bandages. All in all, it was a splendid, brawny, rampaging era, and if I could believe more than two words of it, or if somebody would take the trouble to write even a *tiny* series about it with some pretence of accuracy, I would watch it with the greatest interest, and be vastly entertained.

As it is, I have studied "Wells Fargo," "Wagon Train," "Gun Law," "Cheyenne" and "Sheriff of Cochise" until I am deaf in one ear and have a tendency to walk like a gorilla in high-heeled boots, and I have to report that the only things that have improved since the days of Tom Mix and Buck Jones (you won't remember them either) are cutting, lighting, set construction and fist-fights. The stories are the same old well-thumbed classics of the silent screen. The heroes are the same handsome slit-eyed prigs, and the horses have the same preposterous knack of galloping in and out of buttes, bluffs and canyons all day without falling down dead with exhaustion.

There is music now, to whip up emotional crises, while in the dialogue department characters are apt to come out with stodgy lumps of liturgical chant such as "Guess a man needs a woman, Hank, same as a woman needs a man. Way I figger, that's how it's always been, that's how it's always gonna be." (Solemn chord. Hero brushes away a tear. Sunset over heap of corpses. Titles, credits, signature tune, stand by for ad for furniture polish.) Personally, I quit. Way I figger it, I'm saddle-sore.

HENRY TURTON

Virtuous Circle

When I was young, when I was young
  when I was born in the year '03
the fame of Freud, the name of Jung
  were wholly unsung in the North Countree:
    strait was the way the sinner
      (if ever he dared to) trod:
    Father's descent to dinner
      foreboded the wrath of God:
  not because his love was frugal—
  Father hadn't read McDougall.

When I was young, when I was young
  in the first decade of the centuree
my mother taught me my mother tongue,
  Church Latin, the flute and the Rule of Three.
    With the flat of her hand, when I was one
      she taught me the Wrong which I shouldn't have done:
    with the flat of her hair-brush, when I was two
      she taught me the Right which I ought to do—
  a sound foundation for plant ecology
  Scripture, good manners, and Greek mythology.

Now I must make confession—
  they did not know of the Id:
due to its savage repression
  I loved my mother, I did:
    My complexes shudder like jellies—
    here, here is a thing to perplex:
    they hadn't read Havelock Ellis—
    they *had* read *Œdipus Rex*.

'*Now, do you want to stick,
or go for the next question?*'

The sad years fled, the bad years fled,
  and I was wed, and the children came:
My wife, who had suffered as I had, said
  "We will teach them nothing of shame or blame."
    "Bring up the little clots on
      E. B. C. Jones," I agreed,
    "Let them behave like Watson—
      that is, if they learn to read."
  And soon their little libidos
  began to blossom like the rose.

As we grow old, as we grow old
  in the middle years of the centuree,
long ago they have left the fold
  and our children love neither their mother nor me:
    the Court has rescinded Jill's divorce
      (their father is keeping the kids, of course);
    Tom nevermarried to begin with
      and is kept by the girl he lives in sin with;
    our only grandson—which is odd—
      fears both of them like the wrath of God:
  the child is taught at his mother's knee
  Church Latin, the flute, and the Rule of Three,
    Scripture, good manners, and plant ecology
    but—because of its morals—no Greek mythology.

R. C. SCRIVEN

Times and Customs

PURBRIGHT's wife was having tea with her son in the kitchen. She was eating lardy cake and watching through the window a coal-tit eating coconut above the bird-table. Her son was talking. "Dr Bronowski explained relativity again on television last night," he was saying. "Again I grasped the theory clearly, in spite of the trouble he gets into with his dummy clocks. What time it is depends on where you are. Your weight depends on the speed at which you are moving. Your speed depends upon what time it is. Your whereabouts depends upon your weight. But what is true for you of you is not true of you for anyone else—let's call him 'him'. And what is true for him of him is not true for him of you." He paused. "And I think it gets worse if you are both moving," he added.

"Jonathan," his mother said. "I shall need your help after tea. Your grandmother's grandfather clock will arrive from Dublin at any moment now and your father at about five o'clock." She took a bite of lardy cake, sighed through her nose, and swallowed. "The conventional five o'clock," she said. "The one we all use about the place here."

"I was going to go and have my hair cut."

His mother looked at his head and hesitated. "No," she then said. "A grandfather clock is more important even than that hair-cut."

The door-bell rang. The boy went out and came back with a customs officer. "This is the customs officer," he said. "He has come about the clock."

"I have to sight it," said the customs officer. "It's come from Dublin. My name is Burke. I hope I'm not intruding."

"You mean there may be contraband in it—gold, jewels, evil white powder to test by taste?" asked Jonathan.

"I have to sight it," the customs officer said. Purbright's wife gave him a cup of tea and they sat themselves down round the table.

"As it's my grandmother who sent it," said Jonathan, "you'd better have a good look inside that clock. For her age and weight she is the ablest smuggler in County Monaghan. It is the relaxation of her riper——"

"The boy has not yet learnt the need for tact with customs officers," said his mother. She rose and began to clear the table.

The customs officer turned gravely to Jonathan.

"You need tact with us," he told him. "There was a young sailor at Devonport declared six pairs of real silk stockings. They *were* real. I told him they were imitation and that he need pay only the lower rate of duty. He said I was insulting his stockings. He insisted they were real silk. I charged him the higher duty." The customs officer finished his cup of tea and stood to dry the dishes Purbright's wife was washing.

'*If I want to go up and you're up, do I press the up button because I want to go up, or the down button to call you down to take me up, and if you're down and I want to go down, do I press the down button because I want to go down or do I press the up button to call you up to take me down, and if I want to go up and you're down do I . . .*'

67

The house shook. "That's the clock," Purbright's wife said. Jonathan went out. The customs officer hung up his tea cloth and followed him. A removals van darkened the street. Two men lifted out the long clock and bore it into the house. It was too tall for the hall and they leaned it against the wall. They went out again.

"It's taller than the hall," the boy said.

His mother came quickly from the kitchen. "No!" she exclaimed. "But we checked the measurements with your grandmother . . ."

"A yard is not the same length everywhere," said Jonathan. "Last night Dr Bronowski——"

"Do you mind if I sight the clock now?" the customs officer asked, producing a torch.

"Please do." Purbright's wife looked across into the dining-room, which was an extension of the hall. "The ceiling in the dining-room is a few inches higher. It would be all right in there if it fitted."

The customs officer put his torch back into his pocket. "We'd better take it in there and try it for height," he said. "I can look at it in there." He and Jonathan carried it into the dining-room. A removals man returned and placed upon the table three weights, some lengths of gut, and the pendulum. Purbright's wife chose a corner and they tried it there. It fitted with an inch to spare. The clock looked well in its corner: plain old black oak, its pleasant face set at two o'clock. The second removals man arrived and put an object on the table beside the pendulum. "It goes on top of the clock," he said. He looked up at the clock, standing there as high as the ceiling. "But not in here," he added. He looked at Purbright's wife. "It'll be in your attic for ever more," he said.

After the removals men had gone the customs officer began clock-sighting, and the boy and his mother examined the object on the table.

It was a kind of clock's crown. An oaken frame supported a brass globe and on the globe there perched a small lectern eagle. It occurred to Jonathan that the globe and its eagle unscrewed, as with the brass knob of a bedstead. The customs officer joined them. "Nothing in the clock except the maker's name——" he began, and then the globe caught his eye. He went closer and grasped it. It did unscrew. He took it to the window and stood with his back to the others. He took a notebook and pencil from his pocket and seemed to make a note. He brought the globe and eagle back and began to screw it on again. "A blank," he said. "I've drawn a blank."

"Are you sure——" Jonathan began, and then stopped.

"You were going to say something?" the customs officer asked him.

68

"I'm very young," Jonathan said. "Ideas for things to say are apt to bubble up. Adolescence. But I choke them back."

The customs officer took his leave and Jonathan at once asked if he might unscrew the brass ball.

"You'd better wait until your father——"

The door opened and his father came in. "A customs officer so far inland can only mean one thing," he said. "What has my mother been up to?"

"She's sent the clock," his wife said. "The customs officer was sighting it."

"May I unscrew that brass globe?" the boy asked.

"It's in the dining-room," said Purbright. "I thought it was to go in the hall."

"Too tall."

"But it was measured."

"Your son says that a yard in Ireland is not necessarily the same as a yard here."

"Let's get it going," said Purbright briskly. He took off his coat. "Let's lay it on its side and wind its guts in." He rubbed his hands together.

"You're very brisk," his wife said.

"Touch of frost outside," Jonathan said. "He'll ease off shortly. Now may I please unscrew that globe?"

"He thinks there's contraband inside it," his mother said. "He nearly forced the customs officer——"

"You want to be very tactful with customs officers," his father told him "There was once a young sailor at Devonport——"

"I know," said Jonathan. "But please, please, may I unscrew the globe?"

"Certainly not," said his father. "We must get this clock going at once. I want to hear whether it still strikes six at ten past six. At six it used to pause after the chimes and then, ten minutes later, suddenly strike out." He looked at his watch. "It's twenty past five now. We'll have to work fast."

The old clock protested with faint janglings as Purbright and his son laid it on its back and opened it up. Its insides were not unlike the tops of three tennis-net posts: the gut had to be wound upon brass reels with ratchets, one for each weight, all three almost inaccessible. It was ten to six before each cylinder had its gut wound on. It was five to six before the clock was up in its corner, its pendulum fitted, its weights suspended.

"Suppose I unscrewed the globe now?" suggested Jonathan.

"No," said his father. "Zero hour is upon us. I must now bring the hands forward from two o'clock, quarter by quarter." He moved the hand on to the

HARGREAVES.

quarter-past and a fragment of shaky Westminster chimes sounded. "Hear that?" he said. The sound brought his wife from the kitchen to which she had retreated. She and Jonathan watched as the hands went round, and the clock chimed and boomed. Purbright looked at his watch again. "It's six," he said and brought the hands almost to six o'clock. He pushed the pendulum. The clock began to tick. It whirred within and chimed the four quarters. There was silence. "There you are," said Purbright. "It's waiting," He stood back. "If there's one thing I can handle it's a grandfather clock."

The boy was gazing at the second hand of the clock. "Look," he said, awed. "Look at it. The whole thing is going backwards."

"Nonsense . . ." began Purbright, and then he saw the minute hand jerk back from one-minute-to to two-minutes-to. He tugged at his nose. "I wound on that gut widdershins," he said. "That's what I did. I wound——"

"Dr Bronowski would like this clock," said Jonathan. "This clock is really *for* that doctor."

The telephone rang and Purbright's wife answered it. She listened for a time. She put her hand over the mouthpiece. "It's your grandmother from Dublin. She says there's a present hidden for you in the globe. She wants you to have them because your great-grandfather's initials were the same as yours."

Jonathan leaped for the globe and unscrewed it. Inside were two gold cuff-links, thin with age, a monogram of his initials on each. "There's a note with them," his father said, peering. "It'll be from your grandmother." In the background his mother was delivering a blow-by-blow account to Dublin. He picked out the piece of paper. " 'There is no duty on these valueless gewgaws'," he read out. "It's signed 'R. Burke, Customs Officer'," he said. The clock struck ten-to-six.

A. H. BARTON

The New Vocabularianism

A SENSITIVE gentleman in one of Henry James's novels exclaims at the end, triumphantly, "Then there we are!" not because he and his fair companion have arrived at a solution of anything but because they have come upon an embraceable impasse.

The expression Embraceable Impasse (I stress it with capitals deliberately) might well become a part of the jargon of today's diplomacy, which so often seems content to settle for a phrase in place of a way out. One such phrase, Calculated Risk, has been going great guns among the politicians and statesmen. It was used repeatedly a few weeks ago by an adult guest on an American radio discussion panel made up of juveniles. (I am glad and eager to announce that we have millions of teenagers in America more interested in using their minds than in brandishing knives or bicycle chains.) Finally one youth interrupted the adult to say "I don't know what you mean by Calculated Risk". The grown-up was as bewildered as if the youngster had said "I don't know whom you mean by Harry Truman". This particular Calculated Risk was being applied to the Russo-American plan of exchange students, and the adult guest floundered a bit in trying to explain what he meant.

Now I have made some study of the smoke-screen phrases of the political terminologists, and they have to be described rather than defined. Calculated Risk, then, goes like this: "We have every hope and assurance that the plan will be successful, but if it doesn't work we knew all the time it wouldn't, and said so."

There is, to be sure, a kind of menacing Alice-in-Wonderland meaninglessness in a great deal of modern political phraseology. What used to be called a tenable position could now often be called, quite fittingly, a Tenniel position. To add to the unmeaningfulness of it all, there is the continual confusing contribution of the abbreviationists. We have in America a product called No-Cal, short for No Calories, and another Decaf, meaning "coffee from which caffein has been removed". Before long, I fear, Calculated Risk will become Cal-Ris, and then all the other celebrated phrases will be abbreviated, for the sake of making even less sense than before in front-page headlines. We shall have to have a special glossary, perhaps, to help us figure out Pea-Cœx and "Ag-Reapp" and "Mass-Retal".

I should think even the most backward student of world affairs would understand "Sum-Con". Then the Marxist intellectuals will hit them with those old brickbats called Obscurantism and Obfuscationism. The meaning of these two words will be described, in my own forthcoming dictionary, like this: "You are seeking to distort our objectives by exposing them to the scrutiny of the unfairest of all bourgeois virtues, namely truth".

Somewhere in my proposed lexicon I shall have to wedge in what a lady said to me when I told her I was writing a short piece about the time, if any, of Man on earth. She said, with a distressed sigh, "So much has already been written about everything that you can't find out anything about it".

The brain of our species is, as we know, made up largely of potassium, phosphorus, propaganda, and politics, with the result that how not to understand what should be clear is becoming easier and easier for all of us. Sanity, soundness, and sincerity, of which gleams and stains can still be found in the human brain under powerful microscopes, flourish only in a culture of clarification, which is now becoming harder and harder to detect with the naked eye. My dictionary, in attacking or circling about the terminology of the declarificationists, will contain such directives as this, for the bewildermentation of exchange students on all sides: "When you find that they are superior to us in any field, remember that their superiority is inferior to ours".

Let us mourn for a moment the death of Latin in American high schools. That ancient sword of Cicero, lyre of Catullus, and thunder of Virgil has become the pallid valet of the lawyer and the doctor, laying out their double-breasted polysyllabics, workaday clichés, and full-dress circumlocutions. "I had to let my secretary go," a doctor told me. "She could never remember the Latin for cod liver oil." In my day, Latin was taught in high schools to prepare the youthful mind for the endless war between meaning and gobbledegook. But it was a mental discipline, and discipline has become a bad word in America, for the idiotic reason that we identify it with regimentation, and hence damn it as Communistic. Recent surveys in my country indicate that Latin and certain other difficult subjects were eliminated from school curricula because they were simply too hard for Junior and his sister to understand, and interfered with the cosiness of their security. An aroused America is now, I am glad to say, interested in the rehabilitation of our declining educational system.

The tendency of tired American businessmen and statesmen to use slang and slogan will, I hope, disappear with the revival of true education. When our President recently used the word "gimmick" for "political device" he seemed to open the door for a flood of Hollywood shibboleth. I can only pray that Washington does not fall into the use of "switcheroo" and "twisterino".

My concern about the precarious state of the English language in the hands or on the tongues of politicians shows up in recurring nightmares. Like all precision instruments, English meaning can sometimes be completely distorted by the change of a single letter in a phrase or sentence. "The gates of hell shall not prevail" was once changed in a story of mine to "The gates of hell shall now prevail". In the same way then, "Don't give up the ship" could become "Don, give up the ship". It was after brooding upon these perils that I dreamed one night I was at some kind of Sum-Con, and two famous lines, one English, the other American, became garbled slightly and unfortunately conjoined. They were Tennyson's "Beautiful Evelyn Hope is dead," and that proud boast of all New England inns, "George Washington slept here". They came out in my nightmare like this: "Beautiful Evelyn Hope is deaf. George Washington slapt her."

"Gentlemen, this means war," said a grave voice in my dream, and I woke up. It was hard to get back to sleep, and I thought many thoughts. I began worrying again about the death of Latin, and I said aloud, waking up my wife, "What does he know of English who only English knows?" The restoration of Latin in our schools is not going to save Man from himself, to be sure, but it would help in the coming struggle for a world regime of sense and sanity. *Hoc est*, at any rate, *in votis*.

JAMES THURBER

'*Of course we can't put the hood up—we'll get soaked if we stop.*'

'Are you a believer in long engagements?'

'You have such lovely eyes . . .'

'Cooney's Cassocks stand the test,
Choosy Churchmen say they're best.
Sure-fire sermons, never flops;
Cooney's Cassocks are the tops.'

Diary of a Communal Lady

Translated by ALEX ATKINSON

These recently acquired fragments of a private journal throw a vivid light on day-to-day events in a new "People's Commune" of Red China.

WEDNESDAY. A joyful day. Our village communal kitchen was at last declared open by an emissary of the Great Wise Father Mao Tse-tung, who had travelled far to visit us. Eleven thousand villagers cheered by numbers as the first ton of communal rice was poured into the boiler, the other thirty thousand being on the day shift planting potatoes. (Soon the whole of Ho Shun province will be under potatoes, with a border of bean-shoots a mile wide. True, it was hard work flattening the two sacred mountains in the north-east corner, but we worked with a will for a whole afternoon, and now the province is as smooth as a chess-board. Next year we will have enough potatoes to last the village nearly a month.) Two wives inadvertently fell into the boiler with the rice, in a trance of joy.

Thursday.—The communal kitchen began serving the evening meal at breakfast time, and the queue of villagers stretched twelve deep away to the horizon. It was a heartening sight. This great boon will release us women from useless household chores, and today I started work on the blast furnaces. What bliss! Thirty-seven hundred of us manufactured

'*I'll say this much about the Mao regime—it's given us a great deal more to be philosophical about.*'

three blast furnaces each before sunset, in the big field, and tomorrow they will be in full production. Little had I realized, in the days of my indolent youth, when I made a pretence of being happy painting fans and playing the flute in the summer house of my father, how quickly and economically pig-iron can be manufactured, if you set your mind to it. I am in charge of those who work the bellows— nine hundred and eight grandmothers. As we work we sing the poems of our great Leader-poet, Mao Tse-tung, from the song-sheets provided. At the end of the day the song-sheets are collected by the prefect, Lo Hin, and counted.

Friday.—Memo. I must remember to denounce my mother as a dangerous reactionary. Thrice last week she spat during announcements on the village loud-speakers—once in the middle of a hymn to Mao Tse-tung composed by three quarters of a million seven-year-old children in Chi-Si province, and twice while the assistant Under-Leader of Callisthenics was reading the list of absentees from communal netball, who have since been very properly minced for fertilizer. Also she has refused to erase the pince-nez she scrawled on the tinted photograph of our revered Mao Tse-tung which hangs in the state-certified sleep-room of our allotted dwelling-box. And last Tuesday she refused point-blank to wear her regulation blue denim boiler-suit and peaked cap for her work in the village pig-sties. As the eight thousand pig-sty shock-troops marched off at dawn, their lanterns flickering in the dusk and their voices raised in the joyous chant "Mao Tse-tung the Fattener of Pigs will Lead Us Into Australasia e'er the Blossom has Waned on the Collectivized Soya Bean Bushes," mother brought up the rear in a pair of old striped pyjamas, shouting rude quotations from Confucius at the authorized passers-by. I also happen to know that she is secretly engaged on a work of fiction. From what I have read of it so far it appears to be nothing more than a loathsome anthology of deviationist propaganda. The New China has no room for old women of ninety-three who yearn for such counter-revolutionary luxuries as Privacy, Un-organized Leisure, Personal Ownership of Objects, Freedom to Weep in the Streets, or Family Life. I have given her seven hundred Marxist pamphlets and kept her without food for a month, but still she persists in tuning in to *The Ed Sullivan Show* and

What's My Line? Nothing can remain but liquidation.

Monday.—A gala occasion! At eleven o'clock this morning every villager was permitted to explode one fire-cracker at a signal on the village whistle. This was a mark of joy at the fact that the Blessed Liberator himself, the All-wise Mao Tse-tung, was paying our tiny village a surprise visit! All through the week-end the inhabitants had been kept busy stitching three million flags and banners in readiness for the great day. At noon our Leader appeared on the rostrum which had been constructed in twenty-five minutes by two thousand six hundred members of our local branch of the Affiliated Red China Infant Storm Troop Volunteers. The infants themselves were given leave of absence from the Greetings To Mao Tse-tung Ceremony so that the State-Permitted Clinic of the Heavenly Balm could attend to the whip-marks on their backs—the glorious evidence of their devoted labours. The Great One read to the assembled multitude (three quarters of a million souls from this village alone, and coach-loads of nosey-parkers from Hi Pin province on an Organized Trip) the latest pig-iron and steel production figures, the number of usable babies born last month (a record), eight of his recent poems, and a speech in which he explained how in ten years' time the entire surface of the earth would be covered with citizens of the New China up to a depth of three feet. "And then," he said in conclusion, "we shall see what we shall see!"

Our dwelling-box seems quieter today. Mother's clothes fetched two yen on the black market. I hope no gossiping neighbour watched the transaction, for it seems you can trust no one in this hole.

On Becoming Man

I WELL remember how the race began.
 I was, as I recall, a kind of fish,
But some strange fancy told me to be man.
 The course of things responded to my wish.

And shortly I was sprouting arms and legs,
 And straightening out my unaccustomed spine.
True to my vow, I gave up laying eggs;
 I hunted sometimes, when the day was fine.

I took the dog for friend, and tamed the cow,
 And learned to write, despite the mental strain,
And never told my friends and neighbours how
 I sometimes longed to be a fish again.

R. P. LISTER

'Make up your mind.'

Eat More Peat

WHEN the Americans, the good Samaritans of the nuclear age, brought aid to Ireland after the second world war their officials grew puzzled and pained by the apparent indifference of the Irish to the blessings of modern civilization. Scratching their heads to think of something for the Irish to export, with a view to balancing a precarious economy, they hit upon Irish whiskey, for which they had quickly acquired a taste.

"See here," they said to the Irish, "export more of your whiskey, and then you can import more automobiles and more refrigerators".

But the Irish failed to get the point of this. They would rather, they replied, drink more of their whiskey, and import no automobiles and no refrigerators at all. So the American officials went sadly away.

That was some ten years ago. Revisiting Ireland the other day I saw signs of an economy now grown so unbalanced that the poor Irish can no longer afford to drink all the whiskey they need. Scratching my own head, as I travelled, to think of some other commodity which they might export, and so remedy this deficiency, I reached the bogs of County Donegal—and there hit upon the obvious solution. I hit upon peat; upon little else, in fact, on every hand, but peat. For Ireland is made of it.

Now America, once New England and then New Holland, has been all the time, in a sense, New Ireland too. The Americans even speak with an Irish lilt in their accents, and use Irish phrases long since defunct in England. Why then, with the Samaritan goodwill which this affinity induces, should the Irish not be encouraged to convert Irish peat into American dollars and American dollars into Irish whiskey?

The Americans, far more than the English, are a Conservative people, with a love of all that is sweetly old-fashioned. In their homes, for example, they display a love for the open fire-places of bygone days. A friend of mine once let his London house to some Americans, and the first thing they did was to dismantle his elevator and unbrick his grates. In Texas one August, in a millionaire's mansion, I myself found a log-fire burning merrily on the hearth, nicely taking the chill off the air-conditioning.

In New England and in the millionaires' suburbs of New Jersey and Connecticut I always relished the oak-beamed barns gleaming with antique things—the horse brasses, the ships' lamps, the platters of pewter, the warming pans of burnished copper, and above all the spits which turn over the wide open, ingle-nooked grates, filling the air with fragrant wood-smoke. Why not, I now asked myself, peat smoke, wafted in waves of nostalgia from the Irish bogs?

For a start, I suggest to the Irish that they distribute, as sales samples, peat parcels, gratis to every Westbound passenger leaving Shannon Airport. A demand for peat thus instantly created, they should start to convert their trawlers—for they hate sea-fishing anyway—into peat boats. Quite soon they will have a fleet of them, which should sail at regular intervals not to New York but to such Old New English ports as Bridgeport, Connecticut, Boston, Massachusetts, and Portland, Maine. The cost of transport will be high enough to put peat at a premium, thus ensuring a ready sale as soon as the excited cry goes round the suburbs and exurbs: "The Irish peat fleet's in!"

In no time, in all the richest houses, "Cook on Peat" will be the rule. Peat grills will replace charcoal grills. Peat barbecues, providing peat-flavoured steaks for the guests, will sweep fashionable America from coast to coast. Peatier Living will prevail ("It's more gracious, it's different"). It will be fun to go peaty. There will be Togetherness in an odour of peat smoke.

Peatwise, a new line of snobbery will slowly develop. Hostesses will come to pride themselves on their vintage peat. There will be good years and bad years, varying according to the Irish rainfall, and connoisseurs will learn to distinguish the subtle differences of bouquet between a Connemara '58 and a Galway '52, matured in bins of Californian oak.

But peat is not only for burning. The Irish are famed for their imagination, and the free use of this, in close concert with the sales organizations of Madison Avenue, will confer upon it other properties as well. The *Oxford English Dictionary* defines it as "vegetable matter decomposed by water and partially carbonized by chemical change". It contains—or so says the *Encyclopaedia Britannica*—carbon, hydrogen, oxygen, nitrogen and an ash which incorporates ferric oxide, lime and magnesia. How much more medicinal can you get?

'Fancy ringing people up at this hour! They might have woken us up.'

Thus Irish peat will surely come to be absorbed, internally, in a variety of pharmaceutical compounds, as a cure for rheumatic, diabetic, diuretic, abdominal, intestinal, pectoral and psychological ills. Its health-giving qualities will be made appetizing to the American public in the form of peat extract for baby foods, shredded peat for breakfast foods, peat juice to counter acidity, compressed cubes for peat soup. Instant Peat, which tastes good, as a mouthwash should, and a peat-mix for sauces and pies. The faint tang of the bogs will pervade the city as New Yorkers suck their peat tablets ("Peat sweetens the breath") smoke their peat-flavoured tobacco ("It's Toasted"), drink their Bourbon with iced peat water (a rich golden brown), and munch their Peatburgers at the drug store or the Chock Full o' Peats.

Nor, I imagine, will they be content with eating and drinking and dosing themselves with peat. They will be wearing it too. Does not the dictionary refer to peat wool ("wool impregnated with peat") and peat flannel ("with peat in its contexture")? Peat fabrics of all kinds will appear on the market. Virgin peat will come to rival cashmere and lamb's wool and vicuna for softness of texture. Luxury peatware, appropriate to all kinds of weather, will breathe the essence of outdoor living.

The well-dressed man in the latest worsteds will smell ever so subtly of peat, wear peatskin gloves and a peatswool pullover, use an after-shave peat lotion, blow his nose on peat-flavoured tissues and sleep on a peat-filled mattress in an apartment made soundproof by the new peat fibres.

77

But the Irish, thus sweetened to the uses of advertisement, will doubtless go further still than this. They will entice the inhabitants of New Ireland back to the peat bogs themselves, first equipping them as health-giving luxury spas. Shannon Airport will require to be extended, with a number of new runways, as the millionaires fly over each year for their peat cures, to soak in the peat-water baths of Connemara, to be encased in the peat-packs of Galway, to sweat out the acids, buried up to the neck in the carbonized, peat-heated bog-baths of Donegal.

And in the evenings, adhering to a strict régime before the peat fires in the pump rooms of their clinical hotels, they will be permitted to add to the waters of the peat wells just one tot of Irish whiskey. No more, for the Irish will be drinking the rest.

LORD KINROSS

SIR,

Let us assure the writer from the New World that Lord Kinross was quite right to say "Instant Peat, which tastes good, as a mouthwash should," etc. Not caring much for this delicacy, *like*, however, simply will not do here. In English, like is not used as a conjunction like as, as like and as are as unalike as you like, and like, therefore, should be restricted to qualifying nouns and such-like. "I like Ike," they may say, but not "I, like Ike talks to Foster, have used a few expletives in my time . . ."—or what you like as I, like Ike, am not like Ike talks, but like Ike, if you like.

Yours faithfully,
J. A. ORDE

Gosforth, Northumberland

SIR,

Lord Kinross's otherwise excellent article, "Eat More Peat," contains a serious grammatical error . . . Lord Kinross has said "Instant Peat, which tastes good, *as* a mouth-wash should." It should read "*like* a mouth-wash should."

Sincerely,
New York   ADELE GREEFF

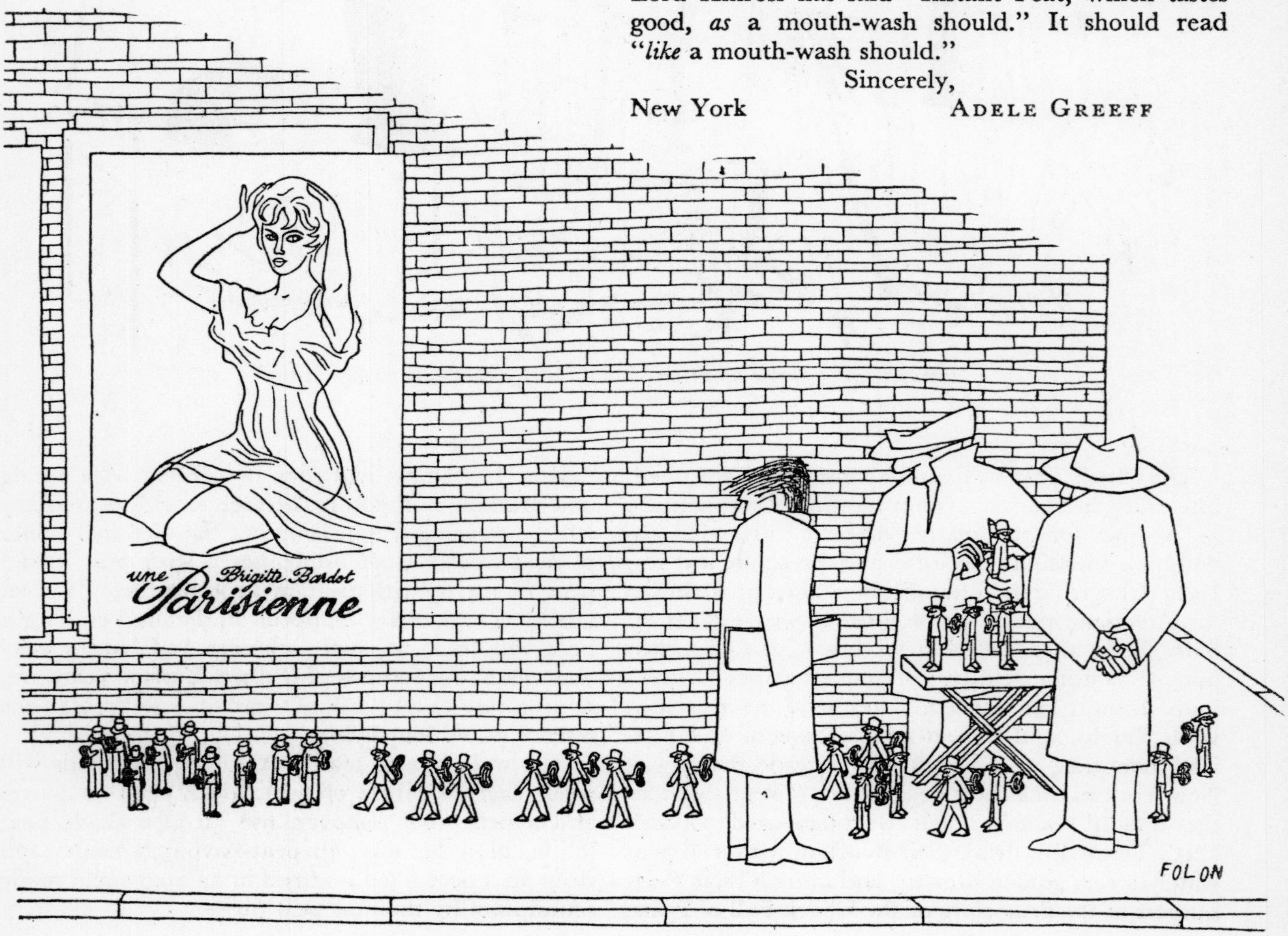

une Brigitte Bardot
Parisienne

FOLON

The Near Thing

WE only met for a moment,
  Beside a lichened wall,
In fact, to be perfectly truthful,
  We didn't meet at all.

The road was a 'B', and narrow,
  The bend was an S, and smart;
I was passing a grocer's van,
  You a pony and cart.

I may have touched the grocer,
  It's hard to be sure, of course:
At an aggregate speed of a hundred
  We certainly scared the horse.

We almost met for a moment,
  Instead we just passed by,
In short, we missed each other,
  Though God alone knows why.

I got half a thumb to the hooter,
  Did you get a toe to the brake?
I reckon a mile between us
  Before we began to shake.

Did the landscape go pink at the edges
  For you as it did for me?
Did you drop to a thoughtful thirty
  For a mile, or two, or three?

We only met for a moment
  (As I think I must have said),
But another moment either way
  And we'd both of us be dead.

And the most alarming aspect
  Of having so nearly met
Is that by this time to-morrow
  We'll both of us forget.

J. B. BOOTHROYD

79

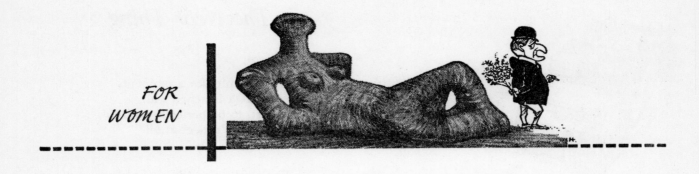

Cold Comfort

AT the first prick of the sore throat which I knew presaged influenza I decided that I must, this time, be ready for it. Usually I totter up and get down stairs, fetching and carrying and sending up my temperature. Morning and evening my husband comes to the rescue; he knows how to make tea and boil eggs.

I got out the car, aspirin was the first necessity but, waiting among the coughing and sneezing customers, I saw that I must also buy gargle, vitamin tablets, glucose, cough mixture, a sedative and a bottle of tonic. Next, as I knew that at any moment my knees might buckle under me, I went to the Supermarket where I could buy everything else under one roof. With one of their perambulator arrangements I went into action, piling in bottles of lime juice and orange squash, tins of fruit juice, two dozen oranges, six lemons, three pounds of butter, three dozen eggs, four pounds of assorted biscuits, a slab of plain chocolate, soap, paper handkerchiefs, disinfectant, and a large melon (which I might fancy during convalescence).

With another trolley I hurried back to the Deep Freeze. This was really for my husband's benefit, but I too might be able to eat a few mouthfuls of chicken by tomorrow. The third trolley was largely devoted to soup. Whenever I am really ill, soup is one of the few things I can enjoy. But my taste is capricious, and if, for instance, I am offered mushroom I long for oxtail. This time there would be no such difficulty. By now I was feeling dizzy, but when the manager and a well-disposed customer had loaded most of my provisions into the boot and stacked the remainder on the back seat I had just sufficient energy left to call at the newsagent's for all the new magazines.

Unloading at home was exhausting for someone in the early stages of influenza, but I was buoyed up by the comforting thought that once in bed I could remain there.

I took all my purchases upstairs and piled as much as I could on to my chest of drawers. Then I cleared all inessentials out and put them into my husband's dressing-room as I needed the space for china, glass, cutlery, teapot and medicines. Even so, most of it had to stand on the floor. By this time I was feeling pretty tired and ill, but one of the tins of soup, some glucose and aspirin revived me enough to move all my husband's belongings into the spare bedroom and make up the bed.

I made a good selection of books and packed them neatly along both window-sills and then made room for writing paper, pen, pencil, stamps, postcards, telephone directory, address book, waste-paper basket, kettle, two saucepans, a packet of detergent, the dish cloth and a tea towel. I fixed a suction hanger to hang up my drip-dry nightgown.

I knew that the doctor was worked to death, so I put off calling him until tomorrow; but as he would arrive after my husband had left to catch his train I tied a long length of string to the spare latch-key; my bedroom window is, fortunately, almost directly over the front door. This also provided the solution to the problem of collecting the milk and bread. I tied a rope to the handle of my shopping basket and practised hauling it up and letting it down.

Filling a kettle at a wash-hand basin is always unrewarding, so I detached the hosepipe from my washing machine and placed that with the rest of the equipment. At the last moment I fetched my knitting, two packs of patience cards, an electric torch and a drawing-board.

Settled in bed, with a tray of tea, two hot-water-bottles, a tin of biscuits and the thermometer, I still found strength to ring up and cancel all my engagements for the rest of the week. I was not sorry to miss the Sale of Work. By the time my husband arrived home I was comparatively cheerful. He squeezed into my room with difficulty, said he supposed I knew what I was doing and offered to boil me an egg.

Worn out, I took a large dose of aspirin and woke, nine hours later, with no temperature, no sore throat and, in fact, no influenza. It took me two days to straighten things out. The oranges and fruit juice and all the frozen food we could not eat were taken round to less germ-resistant neighbours.

It seemed a little hard when one week later, unplanned, unco-ordinated and with the telephone out of action, both my husband and I went down simultaneously with influenza.

BRENDA BROOKE

*　　*　　*

"Competent Secretary required for manager of national firm of provision merchants, age about 23; superannuated position with reasonable hours and convivial conditions; the work calls for alertness and decisive action . . ."

Liverpool Echo

And a steady hand with the black coffee.

'*Absent friends.*'

81

Step Talk

NOT today, thank you. No, really, I mean it. Nothing. Please don't bother to undo your case.

No, no brushes whatsoever, thank you. I have a hair brush. My husband has a hair brush. My daughter has a hair brush. We all share the bath brush. Yes, and we have tooth brushes. Two each, in fact. No, stay . . . I think we are down to five between three now, one has been demoted to doing behind the taps . . . but there is still a jolly mixed bunch in the mug on the bathroom window-sill.

Yes, I agree that it is an exceptionally sturdy scrubbing brush. I bought one last time you came. You remember? That day with the particularly keen east wind? Rather like today, but without the rain?

No, I do not need a back brush, shaving brush, hearth brush, saucepan brush, bath brush or double-sided nail brush.

We peel all our vegetables on principle.

Nor do I want a new soft broom head, though I freely admit that the way the pure bristles spring back after you've stood on them is almost miraculous. Chinese dog bristle? Chinese? Dog? You amaze me. I'd no idea we could still trade with China. How on earth do they get the stuff out over that Great Curtain? I mean Iron Wall?

Really, is that so? What a grasp of world affairs you have. No, I still don't want one. I want nothing at all today.

A free sample of polish? Well, that's extraordinarily kind . . . I hardly like . . . well, thank you.

One moment. What price is that weeny little brush in the corner? Yes, that miniature Christmas tree affair. Isn't it sweet? Three-and-six? I'd like that.

For cleaning out the teapot spout? What a fascinating idea. One so often gets the odd earwig or hairpin straying in, I find. One brisk jab with this little poppet will soon jerk intruders right back in the pot, won't it?

Glad to have seen you. Good day.

D. J. SAINT

* * *

"A little diced cooked tomato can be added just before serving—which should be straight from the frying pan on to the table in the traditional Spanish way."

Edinburgh Evening Dispatch

French polish to follow.

Mummies and Movement

JUMP up, Mummies! This is running music. Run about all over the house as fast as you can. The milk is boiling over, the bath-water's up to the top, there's a frightful smell of burning, the dog's been sick, the iron's on fire. Run like anything, from the baby howling on the sofa to the maniac ringing the front door bell, down two flights of stairs to rescue the washing, up again to the baby who's fallen on his head. Run, run—now stop. Did you run, Mummies? Did you? Good.

Try to make yourself as tall as you can. Stretch up and up and up and up and up. See if you can reach that saucepan on the top shelf without actually dropping the baby or knocking the tray off the sink. Now be as short as short. Feel you are grovelling on the floor picking up rattles, biscuits, shattered china, bootees, bibs—you are? Well done, Mummies.

Let's see if you can make yourself a *strong* shape, a big, strong shape, to straighten out the baby who is bent backwards into a cast-iron hoop and wrestle him into his dolly-sized clothes. Now be a floppy shape. Just flop down anywhere. Let yourself go. Never mind the milkman, the char, the dusting, the dinner, Daddy.

Spread out, Mummies, spread out everywhere, all over the sitting room. Rusks on the mantelpiece, nappies on the wireless, bottle in the fireplace, shawls on every chair, baby powder by the telephone where you took it to answer that kindly soul who never fails to ring up when you're in the thick.

Now sit quietly (it's not for long) and listen to this lovely silence. What do you think it is telling you? Has the baby stopped breathing, choked himself on a fluffy hygienic toy, twined himself up in a Laocoon of cellular blankets, died of a surfeit of tepid groats?

Show me how you can creep. Creep, creep into the bedroom, not a sound, little mice, no light, don't breathe, shoes off, get Daddy to creep too, blast those people upstairs, creep to open the window, creep into bed . . .

Pretend you're a bird, a cloud, a tree, a nutmeg-grater, the dome of St Paul's—absolutely anything but a Mummy.

DAPHNE BOUTWOOD

Height of Folly

On smart stiletto heels I sway,
　　Five inches by a half,
Painfully bringing into play
　　The muscles of my calf.

My sole is wider than my shoe,
　　My toes are packed as one;
My tender feet are black and blue,
　　My arches nearly gone.

But priceless is the elegance,
　　The grace I give my all for,
That wakes the warm, admiring glance
　　In men I am too tall for.

CAROLE PAINE

*'I shouldn't dream of going. I don't like
death-watch beetles.'*

83

The Middle of The Road is No Place to Start Running

TWENTY years back, Juliet—well, let's not push the point, there's the age parallel at any rate; twenty years on, Mrs Exeter, gardening in the right kind of gloves and wearing the right What with the What With No Age-Tag? Forty years on might of course be quite jolly, with a figure that will probably be afar if not absolutely asunder, and a spare half-hour in the evenings to sit down and read when you've finished the washing-up. It's this next ten years that are going to be the roughest.

One of the really terrible things about being in-the-thirties (women stopped sticking at twenty-nine years ago and now take precarious refuge in being in-their-thirties) is that people are often so dreadfully kind to you. If men haven't actually begun to give you their seats on buses again the way they did ten years ago, all the same they look at you with a sort of haunted expression and don't wince when you jab them with your spare shopping-basket. They know it's as much as you and they deserve. In novels you're either worried with four children (Still Young, Still Pretty, poor you) or you're a hard, fast witch in scarlet chiffon with no resident husband and a greedy eye for struggling young architects in tweeds. In the early chapters you seem to be doing all right, but by the middle of the book there's a look of panic behind your eyes. *They* know you're over thirty, and your eyelashes are stuck on with glue. You'll be recklessly downing the martinis in sophisticated Acapulco by the last pages with a no-good playboy oil-king, and the architect will have scuttled back to the little girl with the pony-tail and the dear honest freckles on her innocent (wait for it) *young* nose.

The French have always been particularly kind to

the lady of thirty years, sweetly making believe that twenty-nine is nothing but schoolroom gaucherie and not knowing what to do with your hands and feet, where thirty, suddenly, is a bloom of mystery and enchantment and peach-fed experience. Thirty is the age that knows about witty conversation and discretion between five and seven in the evening and understated little hats and how not to wear scent if you're dining with a man who knows about claret, not that you'd think of dining with one that didn't. Thirty is the lady for whom all the baby couturiers, dreaming of their sainted mothers, build those touchingly fragile little-girl dresses and the pliant, merciless armour that is their all-in-one foundation. Thirty treads very lightly, in genuine custom-built crocodile, because she treads on so many genuine dreams, and often heels them right into the genuine Aubusson.

In bleak moments, in need of cheering up, Thirty often thinks of the Marschallin as her prototype—proud, tender, bitter-sweet, keeping the rules, behaving like a perfect lady, much the most sympathetic figure in the plot.

The woman of thirty-plus is just-an-in-between, too old, except in the novels of Colette, for boys—at any rate for the kind that like a girl to come up smiling at the end of an evening's steady jive, though one wouldn't mind a nice old-fashioned Marchbanks warming one's slippers by the fire when one staggered in from the supermarket—too young for toys like twin-engined knitting-machines and bath-chairs with overdrive. There are so many things she's got to Be On Her Guard Against. Doughnuts, that second martini, finishing up the baby's puréed potato and mashed sardine, primary colours, cheap separates, straggly eyebrows, wandering thoughts, saucepan handles turned outwards, sailor hats, one late night, a hair out of place, getting in a rut, not understanding about *Look Back in Anger*, dressing too young, dressing too old, wrecking her children's chances of happiness in after-life, soaking in the bath eating chocs and reading Daphne du Maurier. At sixteen or sixty you may do as you please, such sins are not mortal. Just about the only things Thirty doesn't have to be on her guard about are the Fascinating Older Man and spots on the chin.

One of the good things about getting so old is that you can talk to yourself by the hour and nobody

'He's walking!'

thinks it odd. What a smashing time you had at twenty-one, all those dances and "In the Mood" and a liberty-cut you could do yourself with a pair of nail-scissors and being so convinced the rich full life of a dramatic critic was going to be a full-time vocation of permanent benefit to mankind.

Your memory's going, it's a sure sign of age. What about paradigms and The Battle of Maldon and the

FOR WOMEN

brutal and licentious medical students and all-white dinners in Hall, pure as a young girl's stainless soul, macaroni cheese, cod and boiled rice?

But there was that delicious moss-green dance-dress . . .

Yes, admittedly that was a bit of luck, curtain-material off the ration with a fade-mark right down the back. We were none of us as bright as that French girl who used to go to dances in her black chiffon nightdress. I think I rather preferred our knee-length pink frilly number with the blue hipline sash and the corals, but that's harking back a bit into the madcap 'twenties. Seems odd we never met Michael Arlen, when you consider how far back we go.

Did we have a nice time at our schools?

Well, the one with the black pudding-basin hats and blue serge knickers was fine, but the one with the green felt hats thought we were a bit weak on House Spirit at times. Probably comes of our Welsh blood. We're not really normal.

I thought it was Team Spirit.

All adds up to the same thing. Character-building, like playing cricket in a blizzard. Trains you for life.

Do you reckon it trained us for that very odd job in Naval Intelligence we never really got the hang of, all those classics dons and Norwegians in huts, and that nice time we had in the B.B.C. before we got so jumpy because nobody ever gave us a deadline?

Of course. It teaches you values and How to Look Up the Facts for Yourself. You can get through most of life with six pairs of white cotton gloves, the collected works of Elizabeth David, and a good basis of classical Latin. Pity we didn't put up a better show as a prefect, though. It would have given us some memories to treasure.

*   *   *

Til crowes feet be growe under your yĕ . . . and calling them laughter-lines isn't going to help anybody on a bright and cruel spring morning. Sometimes, when I wonder which of my remaining limbs is going to fall off next and be swept carelessly behind the sofa, I think of all the things I *can no longer afford to do*. I can no longer *afford* to let a single night go by without cleansing, toning, bracing and nourishing. My skin, on which thirty-four summer suns have fitfully shone and on which the gentle English climate has blasted its traditional gift of the peaches-and-tinned-cream English complexion, can no longer *afford* to be without moisturizing, hormonizing, face-packing and queen-bee-jellifying. The months are whizzing by, already I have lived through two major

diets and accumulated an impressive cultural past. I saw Maurice Evans' Hamlet at the Old Vic when there was such a thing as a pit, and Charles Laughton's Macbeth. Let that sort of thing slip to someone under twenty-five and they start asking you what Irving was like in his hey-day. My musical memories go all the way back to "The Isle of Capri". Sometimes I think I can remember dancing the minuet with my old, old friend Peter Ustinov when we were children and Les Ambassadeurs had a four-piece harpsichord band. That's what happens when you read about action-painters who were born, actually born, in 1938.

The thirty-plus man of course is just beginning to develop some devastating character-lines round the eyes and think seriously about what he is going to do in life. At my age Emily Brontë was dead, Daisy Ashford was a master-novelist many years retired, and Cleopatra had gobbled up several dictators.

There is the odd compensation. Napoleon wrote huffily to Josephine, who had been overplaying her social hand, that no woman under thirty should ever dream of receiving visitors while she was still in bed. Every age, they say, has its special privileges.

SIRIOL HUGH-JONES

'*So this year I said "To Hell with elegance,
I'm dressing for comfort".*'

Parent Ploy

ARE you *au fait* with give-away? Has your child his complement of guardsmen, redskins, skiffle, whistles, marbles, cardboard guns which *really* shoot? Are you up on every package permutation? Or do you still bring home wheatie-crispies (instructional picture cards and the adventures of Tonto) when this week all his heart aches for is crispie-wheaties plus a made-to-measure model (buried, but yes, right at the bottom) of Errol Flynn's yacht?

Can you serve up with a smile rubber bands for plastic space wheels; bicarbonate of soda for plastic submarines; bottles with stoppers for little plastic men in diving suits with that incomprehensible urge to bob eternally up and down? Or do you cry to dear, dear heaven never ever to see another cereal packet again?

Have you the fashionable teeny weeny fingers essential for cutting out a tab-sprouting cardboard model of a zoo animal/vintage car/Pan Am jet clipper? Can you tackle without screaming hysterics instructions to slide slot five into the neck of shape D, inserting tab four in front of swivel hole two, and fitting tab one of shape E into slot A? And what do you do with the glue-and-tear-stained travesty when you've made it?

Has your little one his quota of forty-eight film stars (a free face per packet of bubble gum)? And his bubbly badge? Is he a gumster? Has he his set of Wild West picture cards? Does he belong to the Zip Wide Awake Club? Is he wearing his Ladybird shirt?

Have you done your utmost (2/11d. plus two box-top tokens) to see that he and five of his friends win that once-in-a-lifetime trip to Disneyland, roaming the skies between New York and Hollywood, three whole weeks away from home? I bet you have.

JOAN RICE

Handy Hint

MODERN mothers need the knack
Of a smart, old-fashioned smack
Such as purifies by pain
(Useful in a bus or train).
This is something I have tried
And really *do* feel purified.

ZENA LOWTHSON

The Right Way

JOHNNY! . . .

I won't have you coming into lunch like that! Go outside and come in again, properly this time. Come in at a *gallop* and send the door *crashing* back against the wall.

That's the way.

No, don't pull your chair out and sit down and just pick up your knife and fork. *Throw* yourself into your chair and *grab* your knife and fork as though you're going to attack someone. Like this—

Yes, that's better, but you're holding the knife and fork the wrong way. Hold them like this, as though you have a sword in each hand.

More *aggressively*.

Well, that's better. It's not quite right, but it's better.

Now hold them pointing up in the air and stick your elbows out.

Out.

Right, now start.

No!

Push the knife *and* the fork into your food as *hard* as you can—that's it—*pile* as much on your fork as you can, more than that, go on. No, more than that . . .

Try using it as though it were a spade. Turn it the other way round. Now, *dig*.

Oh, really, what's the matter with you? Why can't you do as you're told? I'm your mother, I'm doing my best for you, I'm working myself to the bone, and this is all the thanks I get. You don't even *try* to learn how to behave. A *baby* would do better.

Now do it again.

Well, all right, that's a bit more like it.

More.

Good boy.

More.

No, don't wait to swallow, just keep pushing it in. That's fine. And keep grinning all the time. Keep your mouth open.

Keep it open!

Push another forkful in.

Faster!

I don't care, you've got to *try*.

What's the matter, don't you *want* me to be proud of you? Don't you *want* to win at the audition and get in a TV commercial?

MARJORIE RIDDELL

Sox and Sockability

(Written after reading the verdict of a secondary-school headmistress that the driving force behind teenage girls is marriage. "Teenage girls today are not so different from the heroines of Jane Austen," she concluded.)

FANNY's heart was sore. The scheme could never commend itself to *her* judgment. *She* could take no pleasure in it. To be walking arm-in-arm across Clapham Common, in full day, no carriage at hand to take them up if clouds should gather, was a plan not very likely to attach her interest or arouse her approbation. But Edmund had given his consent. Edmund had yielded to the inclinations of Maria and Julia. And where *his* scruples found nothing to censure, Fanny must be convinced that her own objections had no weight.

"Where marriage is to be the aim, there can be no imprudence, dear Fanny," said he in a low voice. "I am not now to learn that a young woman, with every advantage of beauty, address and steady employment with the Gas Company, is forbidden to draw attention to her consequence; and that *that* is to be your object in this escapade your luminous socks will sufficiently determine. No, Fanny, to be for ever sitting in your attic, always intent upon your great book of China, always out of society—*there* is indecorum, *there* is self-indulgence, *there* is a fault of temper, a failure of spirits altogether to be reprehended."

So earnest a rebuke, delivered with so much conscious gravity, from one with whom above all others she would chuse to rock and roll, whom alone she permitted to elevate her from the floor and whisk her attentively across his back, could not but make the strongest impression. She would go! She would remonstrate no longer. Happy, approving, it was not in her power to be. But she would go.

'*Your sitter-in wants to know if you believe in corporal punishment.*'

'Before you get up, see if you can find my left eyelash.'

All was soon settled. Julia would wear her three-quarter-length jeans and a start was to be made within the hour. Maria had her seed pearls and was eager to be gone. And Fanny herself, finding that Edmund had taken his flick-knife and set off about some business of his own, had no longer any thing to detain her.

The three young women walked in silence for some minutes, enjoying the mild air, until Fanny, who could not long be unappreciative of the varied manifestations of nature, struck out thoughtfully in the direction in which her thoughts had for some time been tending.

"I am glad to see the evergreens thrive," she remarked, colouring slightly at an involuntary recollection of the last occasion upon which she had found herself in a shrubbery.

"Oh, as to that," Julia replied, tossing her pony-tail, "I believe I am no less sensible of the beauties of the neighbourhood than another. But where are all the men?"

Fanny shrank from what she felt, she knew, to be an injudicious question, and made no reply. Maria, who had been humming an air for which she had a rage, broke off immediately to say, with an affectation of inconsequence that deceived neither herself nor her companions, "Now that we have come so

far, why do we not saunter to the Assembly Rooms? My aunt was observing, if I recall, that Tommy Crawford was to be there this forenoon, and would indulge his audience with a song."

Tommy Crawford! Fanny's cheeks reddened with shame as she asked herself what Edmund would think if he should come to learn that she had permitted herself to be a party to so objectionable a proposition. With Mr Crawford himself she had no acquaintance. They were not in the way of meeting. But she had heard her uncle declare "I am given to understand that he has a talent," and the words, even without the look of scorn that accompanied them, were enough. But what could she do? What objections, what remonstrances could she urge that would avail against Maria's reckless determination, Julia's willing complaisance? Her heart was heavy but she bent her steps in mute agitation towards the Assembly Rooms.

It was worse, much worse, than she could have imagined. All was heat, confusion, impropriety. Fanny felt herself oppressed. She was near to fainting. Maria and Julia pressed forward, however, into the thickest of the throng, until they stood within the inner circle of hep cats surrounding Mr Crawford, and Fanny, fearful of being left unattended in such a place and anxious, if an opportunity arose, to restrain her cousins' indelicacy, could not but follow them. Of Tommy Crawford himself she caught but a glimpse, for his admirers, in their eagerness to recommend themselves, very soon threw him to the ground and began to possess themselves of fragments of his clothing. This was bad, very bad. But astonishment and disgust gave way to real mortification when she observed Julia, her jumper in disarray, seize hold of Mr Crawford's tie and wrench it without introduction or apology from his neck. Fanny would, *must* speak.

"Reflect, Julia," she cried, unconsciously echoing Edmund's words. "Where marriage is to be the aim, there can be no imprudence. But *that* justification for your present indulgence you will scarcely, I imagine, pur forward. If consideration for your own feelings of delicacy have no weight, will you not at least spare Mr Crawford the pain of separation from an ornament that sentiment and a modest desire for decorum may well combine to make him cherish? I beg, I pray you to lay off."

Julia herself, after a moment's thought, made no reply. To Maria, feverishly placing a waistcoat button, with a look of conscious triumph, in her reticule, Fanny recognized that it was useless to appeal. There was nothing to be done. It was all misery—all, all lost.

Fanny's one thought, one prayer, was to be alone. Only a shrubbery could help her now. But one final vexation, a last bitter wound yet awaited her. Mr Crawford roused himself. He threw off six or seven of his closest attendants, and supporting himself upon an elbow fixed his gaze, an eager, questioning gaze, upon poor Fanny.

"Who is that square?" he asked.

That he should dare—! That she, who had long deemed herself the equal of any Jane Austen heroine—Fanny gave herself up to sixteen pages of mortifying reflections.

H. F. ELLIS

'*Nobody's dead!*'

Bedtime Story

OVER the set the sleeping-net;
    Over the cheek the pack;
Over the arms, the wrists, the palms,
    The cream to cure the crack.

Under the skin beneath the chin
    The lotion bloom enhances.
Beauty must sleep extremely deep
    Under the circumstances.

HAZEL TOWNSON

Lay That Pistil Down

"Facts of Life." Father of boy and girl would deeply appreciate a beautifully written essay on this subject.—The Times.

You must have noticed that often when a lady and gentleman kiss on the pictures or TV it is not the same sort of kiss that you give your Mummy and Daddy, or even the same sort that Mummy and Daddy give each other. This is one of what we call the facts of life, just as girls and boys have different bicycles. They are different in other ways, too, though not as different as they used to be before jeans were invented. And, by the by, do not confuse jeans with genes, because these were invented much, much earlier, though you have only just begun to hear about them on the B.B.C.

I know you are very interested in birds, and love to see the blue tits hanging upside down from a half coconut, but I am sure you know that it is cruel to take their eggs—because if those eggs are left to ripen they will have other birds in them, and in time *they* will hang on half coconuts and *they* will have eggs with other birds in them. Yet there is a difference between the bird and the coconut, which does not have eggs but is a native of the Malay Arch-i-pelago, whence it has been carried by human agency to tropical and subtropical regions in all parts of the world. Perhaps you can most easily associate the word "coconut" with the word "shy", and if so I am very pleased as shyness was the next thing I was going to talk about.

Little boys and girls are very often "shy" with one another, though not, of course, if they are brothers and sisters. When it comes to the facts of life, brothers and sisters are not boys and girls in that sense at all, but often ride each others' bicycles and think nothing of it. I expect you have noticed, too, that a boy throws a ball at a coconut shy quite differently from a girl, except when the girl is what is called a "tomboy". I expect that will remind you of a "tomcat", and it is true that a tomcat is very much more boy than girl, and cannot have kittens, any more than little boys can. Boys often ask their Mummies, "Can I have a kitten?" and do not understand why they are always told "No". It is a fact of life.

One thing that must have puzzled you, since you were about six, was where you were seven years ago?

You ask Mummy and Daddy where *they* were seven years ago and they tell you at once. Twickenham, or perhaps even Esher, but when you ask where *you* were they put you off with e-vas-ive answers. You must remember that even your parents do not know the exact answer to everything, and though there are such songs as "Only a Baby Small, Dropped from the Skies" these are not really giving the facts of life in a true form, as your friends at school may have told you. This does not mean that you should believe all that your friends at school tell you. It is much better to pay attention to a beautifully written essay like this and try to understand what is being said to you.

When a bird . . .

When a cat . . .

I realize that I should have said that coconuts are not the only natives of the Malay archipelago. Many of the natives there are Mummies and Daddies in the same way that your Mummy and Daddy are, exactly. The population was nearly six million in 1947, very unevenly dis-tri-but-ed, leaving large, virtually uninhabited areas of mountain and swamp jungles. When you are older I will lend you some books about the facts of life in that part of the world, by a writer named Somerset Maugham.

Rabbits are . . .

A bee is a fer-ti-lizer, but instead of being spread, like other kinds, it buzzes from flower to flower.

Perhaps the best thing is to think of your Daddy as a great big bee, with only one flower to go at (Mummy!). I expect he has talked to you about the facts of life from time to time, and seemed the biggest bee you ever listened too. If so, remember that that's just what *he* was feeling all the time.

J. B. BOOTHROYD

91

Off Chance

When Man, proud Man, traverses space
  To stars that seem to merit it,
This earth will seem a different place—
  The Meek may yet inherit it.

M. KEEL JONES

Notes from the Provinces

Now that the provinces are quite respectable, literary-wise, and all the reputable publishers are sending their prodigies up for a three-month stint in Nottingham and The Town I Mustn't Name (people have just stopped calling it Stoke round *our* way), it seems an apt time to toss out a memoir or two of those past gilded years when, feckless, handsome, rakish, a gay *flaneur* tossing a mop of wine-dark hair, I trod the boulevards of Nottingham, a key figure in that city's intellectual renaissance.

These were the palmy days after the war (the bit that Cyril Connolly called "closing time in the gardens of the west") and what I want you all to know was that there was just as much despair, and of just as good a quality, in Nottingham as there was anywhere else. Even at that time Nottingham was in touch; there was a constant to-and-fro between it and Soho, and when Dylan Thomas got his finger stuck in yet another bottle we heard about it just as soon as you boys down there. This time constituted a period in itself, the period when people could get grants just for *being like that* and everyone wore leather patches on the elbows of *perfectly new* Harris tweed sports jackets. Nottingham was full of Jewish refugees called Giselda, who wore black stockings and played the harp. It was a kind of provincial Vienna, though rather short on opera and *gemktlichueit*. The Council House, an imposing edifice designed by Sir Christopher Wren, and built in about 1927, adds something distinguished to the town, especially when visiting Mohammedans, mistaking its purpose, go and pray in the shopping arcade.

At this time I worked in a commercial art studio,

'*What assets has your Union?*'

from time to time, in an atmosphere of cautious abandon; that is, we would have liked to have been abandoned, but this was England, and the Midlands, and one could hardly . . . One of the artists, a tall gaunt figure who always carried a bottle of milk in his pocket (on one occasion, on the top deck of a bus, the cap fell off and milk flowed down the aisle and down the stairs. "What's going on up there?" shouted the conductor), was constantly meeting people who told him, because he asked them, how to make money. He grew mushrooms in old pairs of shoes. He gave music lessons. Being, however, essentially good-hearted he had not the power to tell his poorer pupils that never, in a month of Sundays, would they make good musicians; when they came he would hide in an alcove behind the front door, and they would circulate the house, peering in through all the windows, until at last they would go fuming away. The most delightful thing that ever happened to him (for our purposes) was that one evening a man came to his door (he lived in an ordinary house in the heart of an ordinary suburb) with two horses and asked if this was a stud-farm.

All the artists tried to think of ways of making money. For instance, we all drew cartoons and sent them off to *Punch*, which inexplicably returned them; the cartoons all had strange captions that were juicy with subtlety and social significance, and I have one here, characteristic of the period, which shows a married couple of middle age sitting somnolently in front of the fire with the wife saying "I suppose I do look different. I've been run over."

One of our curious discoveries was that in the milk bars of the city there were young men of the same age as ourselves and of much the same disposition who simply did not work. They slept on the pipes in the public library. They were writing pornographic novels in ten volumes that were to be published (in English) in Italy and smuggled back in women's corsets. They read Nietzsche (but then, who didn't?) and cadged drinks in the milk bars. They kept diaries about their phallic selves and every entry began: "The agony continues—unabated."

One of them actually lived in a cave under Nottingham Castle. "Are you normal?" they used to ask people, meaning sexually, but of course what was normal to them was abnormal to other people. If they went to bed, to sleep that is, before four in the morning you knew they were really ill. Like us they were all looking for ways of making money, a curious bourgeois streak; all saw themselves as potential entrepreneurs, building up great business empires

and smoking cigars. One man had an idea for selling tinned beans—with this "twist" (as he called it), that the lid, when wiped clean of tomato sauce, would prove to be a small gramophone record which would pulse forth popular ballads at 45 r.p.m. Another man had the idea for building optical prescriptions into the windscreens of cars for women snobs. Someone else was called Colin Wilson. I always called them the sugar beet generation, because the only work they did was to work in the sugar beet factory at harvest time. By this they made enough to live on for the rest of the year while they created—havoc mostly. Of course they lived on other people's sofas and never spent anything.

It was when the Expresso bars started that the rot set in; it meant that anyone could be like us. It was terrible. The Expressos filled a previously unexpressed social need, to judge from the fact that it drew, from seemingly respectable homes in the suburbs, persons such as had never been seen out before. There were *louche*, beduffeled youths, looking like Marlon Brando and carrying double basses; and damsels with black eye-shadow, stark-white faces, and legs longer than any we had had in Nottingham before. It was all a part of the new continentalism. Characteristically in the van of social changes, I was to be seen each evening supping the frothy ambrosia and peering inquisitively through the fronds at the low necklines of the debby waitresses. They were waitresses such as even cosmopolitan Nottingham had never seen. Delectable and slinkily attired they were actresses "resting", as they put it, or "freelancing". Though they forgot their orders and spent most of their time saying "Daddy was absolutely *livid*" to one another and having their bottoms pinched in dark corners by the more favoured regulars; to be short-changed by one of these geishas was an emotional experience.

In this provincial *demi-monde* I played, I may tell you, no small part. The intellectual society of Nottingham was me. I was the toast of the flappers as I entered these *boites*, immaculate save for a flake or two of dandruff. Outside, the November rain oozed down the gutters. Within we were unaware of it. Maddened by the pulsing of aphrodisiacal Spanish guitars, relayed through the Tannoy, by the heady scent of the tropical greenery that decked the trellises, and the intense soulful hissing of the Italian Gaggia, we lived in another, a continental world. Against this background you could find me in some corner, with a court of followers, pushing the *cher maitre* stuff to its logical conclusion. Behind me the Gaggia worked without steam; I, in my turn, steamed without working, talking of Schopenhauer and commercial propositions.

Intellectual cogency was interspersed with amorous dalliance. I was courting a toothsome, long-legged morsel whose name was not, but would have been had she thought of it, Ernestine. She wore fur coats. She rode all the time in taxis. She smoked exotic cigarettes. She was the sort of girl who liked to

be kissed all the way up the arm to the shoulder. She had a teddy bear that answered the telephone for her. You always felt she had just that moment got off a horse. Her two pleasures in life were ritzing and slumming. We used to go into Sneinton and try to get robbed. All her friends had inflatable lifejackets and, by God, if I'd have had more influence they would have needed to use them. (They went sailing, you understand.)

Ah, whither has gone the visionary gleam? Nowadays things have changed. Everyone is turning Anglo-Catholic and telling you that God doesn't have to exist for people to believe in Him. One meets the sugar beet men occasionally. It is difficult to know what to say about them; most are very respectable, and in a position to afford a lawyer. For us, to marry, to work was betrayal, but now one meets them and they are employed and married and with children; one hardly dare remind them of the time when they threw stones at the register-office because of what it stood for. Occasionally one meets a surviving vagabond, but they are all either just coming out of or going into a mental hospital, or are curiously out of touch; one came up to me with a commercial venture, but it hadn't the vision of our old commercial ventures (he wanted to go round from door to door exchanging new non-iron shirts for old-

fashioned ones, and then *melting the others down;* as I say, he was very out of touch). What happened to the one called Colin Wilson God only knows (those two were always on good terms).

Some of us rejected the lure of the respectable, and went into universities, professional intellectual vagabonds in the thesis-writing world, still trying to meet John Lehmann and not succeeding, still unmarried and not liking it. But the thing is: we were angry before the others even started niggling; we were beat before Jack Kerouac knew one end of a car from the other; we were Zen-Buddhists before J. D. Salinger knew how to spell *Bhagavadgita.* Of course if this were America this strain in the national intellectual tradition would have been written up a thousand times. As it is you must make do with passing chronicles of this sort.

MALCOLM BRADBURY

Gracious Picnicking

COME with the Hitch family on a "different" picnic! Yes, Mrs. Hitch has been soaking up Woman's Page advice and *her* picnic will be sophisticated, *bon vivant,* right away from sandwiches and very much in the mood of 1958!

And happy anticipation is the keynote of that mood as Mr. Hitch unlocks the hired van and out they all spill—Auntie Nell, Uncle Jim, three pounds of diced raw veal, Maisie, some cooking brandy, old Donald with the stove wrapped round his foot and a refectory table to flatten the lot of them into one merry heap!

See the ideal picnic spot Mum has chosen for background to her *haute cuisine.* It took only five hours find as against the normal three and it's got everything. A ruined temple for muted greys and broken vertical effects. Level turf for the Chippendale chairs, a purling stream for a natural wine cooler. See too how Uncle Jim munches quite savagely at the bouquet of *fines herbes* he found down his neck. The fact is that this burly man, accustomed to the regular meals of Glossop Villas, bids fair to jar the leisurely tempo of good eating. Quick, Mum, out with the Martinis!

Mum's picnic Martinis have a tiny squeeze of redcurrant juice for outdoor piquancy. She pours them from a narrow-necked vacuum flask into her finest crystal glasses and carries them round on a lacquered tray, dodging Dad's fight with a huge square of *broderie anglaise* and a blackthorn. How wise to bring her daintiest tablecloth! But the Martinis, for all their tangy slivers of anchovy, do a fat lot for Uncle Jim and turn Auntie Nell downright silly.

"Can't we eat the tea before the lunch then?" she shrills, hitting at the midges. "Surely to goodness the *bread* is cooked?"

D

'Where the devil's that half-bottle of claret?'

"All hands to laying the table!" cries Mum swiftly. "Maisie, the Georgian silver! Dad, the wineglasses, three each! Jim, here's a diagram of how finger-bowls go! Donald, a centrepiece of pretty flowers! And hurry, I shan't be a second with this *Vitello Mainbocher*!"

To make a *Vitello Mainbocher* Mum fries chopped garlic in butter till nicely browned, pops in 2 lb. rice, shakes it for 8 minutes, then covers with a good meat stock, letting all simmer till soft before adding the veal, wine, mushrooms, green peppers, avocadoes, aubergines, lychees, pawpaws and stale bread-crumbs, after which she stirs for 90 minutes. It is an ideal picnic dish. She has got as far as knocking the rice bag over when Uncle Jim, all smiles at the savoury smells, helpfully tips a packet of salt into the *marrons flambes* Mum has planned to follow the Duck Maryland.

"Come on, everybody find thirty different wild flowers! It'll take ages!" shouts Donald, the dear nature-loving boy.

To make *marrons flambes* Mum washes the salt off the *marrons* twice then chucks them in with the garlic and runs up a spotted dick with her free hand. How her head aches! Why is the sun setting? What has Donald found? Some Oxford ragwort. (No one else is play-ing.) He is so excited he falls over the stove and it blows up. Dad goes for a torch. Mum can just see Uncle Jim making off with the raw veal in his handkerchief. Auntie Nell is half-way up the ruin, being swooped round by a bat. Donald has got 346 wild flowers and is on to glow-worms. Mum is mixing sugar, duck-fat and breadcrumbs into little mad rissoles and toasting them over an unlit barbecue. Uncle Jim has found the brandy. Auntie Nell has fallen down inside the ruin. Donald has tamed an owl. Uncle Jim gives the tablecloth a wicked twitch just as Mum flings a lettuce and six table-napkins into the emergency cauldron with an eerie laugh and Maisie——

But what is this wild beast that looms from the undergrowth, a vast, snorting shape in the darkness?

No one ever knows. (They were in Woburn Park, they find later, so it could have been pretty well any-thing.) But what *matters* is that it goes through the place like a steamroller and all they have to do is shovel the debris into the van and beat it. The Hitches know that gracious picnickers leave no litter!

They park on a bit of grass outside some council houses and eat the sandwiches Mum has put together from a saved loaf and a beetroot.

"Nothing like a good plain sandwich eaten in the open air when you're hungry," says Uncle Jim, and all heartily agree. Why don't *you* try the Hitch family's healthy, simple way with a picnic—so "different" from those complicated things everyone's going in for nowadays?

ANGELA MILNE

'Oh goody—here's some ready made!'

School Report

"*TOO* easily satisfied. Spelling still poor.
 Her grammar's erratic. Lacks care.
Would succeed if she worked. Inclined to be smug."
 I think that's a wee bit unfare.

Ah well, their it is! Disappointing perhaps,
 For a mum what has always had brane,
But we can't all have looks or be good at our books . . .
 She's her father all over agane.

CAROLE PAINE

99

Familiar
Faces *seen by*
Emmwood, Hewison
and Ronald Searle

Billy Cotton, Tommy Cooper
and David Nixon by Emmwood

Margaret Leighton
by Ronald Searle

Googie Withers and Sir Michael Redgrave by Ronald Searle

Jacqueline Mackenzie
by Emmwood

Sir Kenneth Clark
by Emmwood

Dame Flora Robson
by Ronald Searle

*Fernandel and
Sir John Gielgud*
by Ronald
Searle

Derick Heathcoat Amory
by Hewison

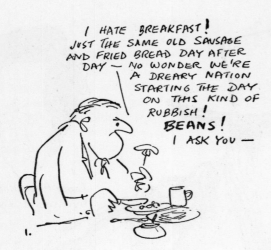

Thoughts on Anti-Matter

A scientist at Berkeley, Cal., has succeeded in photographing a particle of artificially produced anti-matter.

In Berkeley, Cal., a don
  Is making anti-matter;
No sooner made than gone,
  So quick its fragments scatter.

But, reader, do not sniff
  Or ask him why he bothers. Is
His work not worth it if
  It raises this hypothesis:

That where man's furthest sight
  The deeps of space traverses
Conceivably there might
  Be anti-universes?

This theory is appealing
  To most of us, no doubt,
Because we have a feeling
  That things should cancel out—

Beyond the last abyss
  That telescopes can scan it
Is possible there is
  A pleasant anti-planet,

Where, amid learned chatter,
  There works an anti-don
Who's busy making matter,
  No sooner made than gone.

PETER DICKINSON

Chatting with Fido

NOTHING assures us that someone in Peprosverdlodsk is not teaching dogs to talk. If it happens there it will happen here very soon, like satellites. Now is the time to forget for a moment about the sheer marvellous miracle of it all and start wondering "What shall I and my dog talk *about?*"

It's the same kind of worry that held things up a while back when there was all that big prognostication about a radio message from Earth to Mars. Just what were we going to say to Mars as an opener? Who was to concoct this stupendous communication, alerting the Martians to the existence and worthwhile character of the human race? Nehru? H. E. Bates? Bob Hope? Someone chosen at random from the telephone books? The Man from the Pru?

You will want to make a good impression on your dog. The man or woman who becomes known as a conversational flop dog-wise may find invitations to week-ends dwindling.

The question arises, just how sophisticated are dogs going to turn out to be? Their observed habits tell one something—as for instance that they will be but faintly interested in a chat about the bees and the flowers. They know all that.

Indeed it would be wise at the outset to make it a firm rule not to let your dog talk bawdy or smut in your presence. We do not yet know where dogs draw the line, or whether they know about drawing a line at all. Some of his or her experiences, laughable or merely commonplace to the dog, may be embarrassing to you and your circle of friends.

Without actually snubbing him show your dog, too, that you are not interested in his dialect story about the Alsatian, the Scotty and the Dachshund. Do not, on the other hand, discourage him unduly. He may have a keen sense of humour and an eye for comical detail.

The out-of-doors dog may be the one that has the least challenging word-power. But we must all learn to keep our tempers when he starts to assess our capacity with gun or rifle before a roomful of fellow sportsmen. Many dogs have very sharp derisive tongues, and it will be best to start being extra kind to your Spaniel or Setter at once, otherwise he may humiliate you later.

Dogs have a good deal of time for meditation and use it. One sees them lying there on the rug thinking. Soon we shall know what it is they've been thinking

'It won't stop'

103

about. The revelation may not always be pleasant.

Some people when acting as hosts to a dog are ill-advised enough to pretend to know what is on his mind. They see him smile and say "He's thinking of that lovely bone he's going to have later today," or they will attribute his pleased expression to erotic imaginings about his "girl friend" down the street. Such people will stand properly rebuked when Fido finally gets around to speaking to them about the matter. He may forgive them for being apparently gluttonous or sex-mad, but they should not judge others by themselves. When a dog smiles it may be that he is recalling some witty aphorism uttered in jolly company the day before; his air of contentment may be induced by satisfaction with the latest pronouncement of the Transport Commission or an Archbishop.

Beginning now, you should make the effort never to say or do in the presence of your dog anything which you would prefer not to have widely reported. Always look under and into things such as sofas and the back seat of the car, and make up your mind in advance whether it is going to be all right for Fido to stay there or whether it would not be more prudent to lock him up somewhere else for the evening.

Naturally he will tell everyone about how you routed him out from his comfortable observation post, and put the worst possible construction upon your action. It will be for each individual to decide whether he prefers to have that happen or to leave Fido in position and abandon whatever it was the individual had in mind to do.

Your best protection will be to get the dog to share your interests or at least to understand them. Otherwise you may find yourself constantly punished for actions which are natural to you but appear unintelligibly wanton or disgusting to the dog.

Tell him all about your trauma and the potting-shed and Mom. It will help if he at least has some idea of how you got the way you are.

He may like to watch television with you. Encourage this. Dogs on television or the movies almost always have very good characters. They love humans and wish them well. Often enough they will sacrifice their lives to get a human out of trouble. Expose your dog as often as possible to this type of picture. Remark what a wonderful uplift and glow it gives a mammal, however many legs it has, to win the respect and admiration of millions of fellow beings.

Having been without it for so long dogs may tend to over-use the wonderful gift of speech when they get it. Be prepared for your dog to talk all the time, repeating what the weather forecaster said the weather was going to be today, making little comments on everything that comes to his attention —remarking of the United Nations building that it is a very high yet flat-looking building, isn't it? Or that Shakespeare certainly wrote quite a number of plays. If this goes on long enough you may find yourself barking.

All in all, it would be best to accustom ourselves to the probability that the new era of dog speech, in which dogs are going to shout us down, kibitz, make wounding remarks, tell lies and be offended if we do not believe them, is probably not going to be a very happy one for humans. I remember that in ancient Ethiopia dogs got the upper hand to such an extent that it was customary to elect a dog as prime minister. People the dog made signs of not liking were executed, exiled, tortured or at best socially ostracized. And that was before dogs could even speak.

CLAUD COCKBURN

'They're being held up already.'

All the Fun of the Festival

EDINBURGH

SOME go to the Festival by air, looking down when half-way there on a dark peg which is Blackpool Tower and a turquoise which is the South Shore swimming pool. Others make it by steamer from Milford Haven or Etaples or Barrow-in-Furness.

These latter come ashore at Leith while crates of talking dolls and chromed claymores are swinging up and out of the hold. The boys have thin holiday beards, hair like knitted skull-caps, post-Existentialist trousers and rucksacks with Malaparte's *Kaputt*, Professor Burndept's *Social Logistics* and Father Houyhnhnm's *Pastoral Slum Theology* in the outer pouches. Dressed much the same, the girls are identified by their braided blonde hair and eyes of cornflower blue which, speaking for myself, when viewed near the Scott Memorial (say) at 8 a.m., leave me doped and dreamy for the rest of the day.

This is the generation that has given Sartre the slip, the Post-Ex Generation, let us call them. I try to look at Edinburgh through their eyes.

Before us, as we stand on the North Bridge, rise the Castle and its Rock, a brown molar embedded in gums of smirched green. Round the corner now and up the High Street. Steeplejacks have lassooed and bridled the top gilt of St John's cloud-capped spire, which was struck by lightning a month ago; they crawl and swarm terrifyingly on frail ladders and crazy platforms to repair the act of God. From the bagpipes shop below, extant since 1827, comes the squeal of a chanter. We peek through the dusty window. Pipes are being played by a boy behind the counter. Sunlight the colour of saffron and two naked electric bulbs shine on harps, brass-shelled drums, tusks of ivory.

Next, the Camera Obscura. The stairs up to the

viewing loft are clean and bare and smell of baking potatoes. The viewing room is night-black, with two blue lights behind armoured glass.

There it lies, complete and entire, on the beech-wood viewing table, this Royal Burgh and City of Edinburgh. As the man works the periscope handle the Burgh revolves under our noses, segment by segment. Shoppers drift, halt and hasten along Princes Street. A hump of Forth Bridge shows behind a tree-crested hill. A paddle steamer gleams faintly off Portobello. In the shadow of the Scottish Academy a girl in high heels and smart tangerine suit dispenses evangelism from a van like a coffee-stall. Smoke slants from myriad chimneys, seagulls flap tranquilly by, a man in a kilt steps back in the nick of time from the front wheels of a motor-coach on the corner of North Bridge and the Royal Mile.

But what, suddenly, is this, who are these on the cobblestones outside St Giles's?

Six gentlemen slow-march downhill with stern faces, silk hats, morning coats, white gloves and spiral silver truncheons. Can they be the spearhead of the State procession on its way back to City Chambers after inaugural prayers and music in the cathedral? But yes. See the Mace and Sword, the cocked, tricorne and mediaeval hats (a whole flower bed of them) and the ermine capes and the scarlet, brown and puce robes (striped morning trousers underneath) which grandly and majestically march behind.

We are down the Observatory steps in a streak. Tagging along behind the procession's final squad—composed of High Constables and foursomes from the Scottish Actuaries and the Scottish Chartered Accountants—we gate-crash up three flights of steps into an official tea party full of imported mayors or their rough equivalents.

106

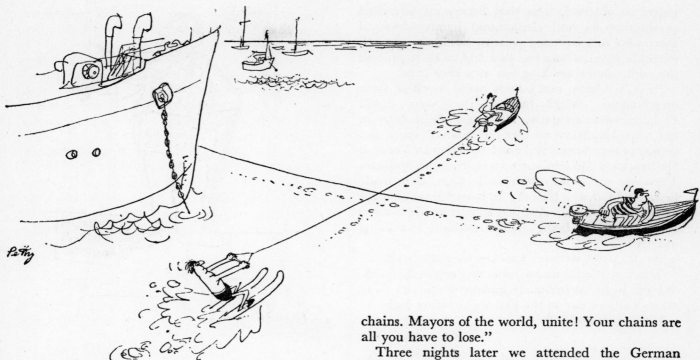

"Why," we ask Zygmunt Dworakowski, President of the Warsaw City Council, "do you wear a chain of office in brass and steel?"

"But it is *not* in brass and steel," says Mr Dworakowski. "It is in gold and silver."

"Then why is it *made* to look like brass and steel?"

The problem, we gather, has puzzled Mr Dworakowski himself a good deal. It wakens him up in the middle of the night.

"Can *you* account for it?" we asked, turning to Dmitri Popov, Chairman of the People's Council of Sofia. Mr Popov, a wavy-haired athlete of forty, turns out his palms hopelessly and shrugs his shoulders so high that it takes him a good ten minutes to get them down again.

"You will notice," interposes Jovan Jankovic, Vice-President of the People's Committee of Belgrade, "that myself I don't wear a chain at all."

"Why so self-effacing?"

"Because," says Mr Jankovic, not intending (we think) to be taken seriously, "if I wore a chain of office citizens would spot me in the street and would shake their fists, saying 'Why don't you build us more flats?' or 'Why is electricity so dear?'"

Somebody else—it may have been the Lord Mayor of Prague or the Burgomaster of Reykjavik—observed: "Mr Jankovic is an exception. Man was born free, but look around you—everywhere he is in chains. Mayors of the world, unite! Your chains are all you have to lose."

Three nights later we attended the German Ambassador's party for the *Euryanthe* singers from Stuttgart. We are too busy being furious about the Moltzau Collection, visual *clou* of the whole Festival, to pay proper attention to the champagne and breast of chicken. Our hearers form a respectful circle. They comprise Klemperer, Ansermet, Sir Compton Mackenzie, Inge Borkh, Wilma Lipp, Art Director Davy Baxandall, a threat of Procurators-Fiscal, a scrawl of Writers to H.M. Signet and young Mr Rasoumovsky, from Germany, a descendant, no less, of that Count Rasoumovsky to whom Beethoven dedicated the string quartets.

We say:

"Renoir? We have seen nudes in the same vein but better painted (of course) on porcelain washbowls offered as prizes on houp-la stalls.

"Cézanne? One of his Bathing Women has a splintered, suppurating left leg. Her friends couldn't care less. Another has a forty-five year old body on ten-year-old shins. Social observation here, right enough. Rickets produced by factory labour in infancy, clearly. But is it, as our fathers used to insist it was, *beautiful?*

"Picasso? Seated Woman 1953 is a lesson in what the human face looks like when run over by a tractor-plough and left out on the window sill to bleach. It is a lesson that doesn't interest us in the least. Woman Seated 1921 has plethoric tendencies, a splendid full-bottomed wig, blood pressure that's nobody's business (not even her dietician's, we regret to observe), eyes that betray an advanced persecution fix and elephantoid hands which, if there were any common sense or humanity around, would be lifted at once by block and tackle to prevent the poor woman crushing her own knee caps.

"Yes, we know our fathers made much of these monstrosities. Why? Because they were dotty. Fathers always *are* dotty. We, too, shall be dotty in our turn. Meantime we take our shoes off daily, put on our prayer jackets and enter the Scottish National Gallery, only three minutes away from the Moltzau. There we see Titian: flesh made satin, satin made flesh. And Goya: a blue sky and a red cloak that are as precious as bread. And Velasquez: an old woman who, as well as being an old woman, is a living oak tree . . ."

At this point we were knocked over the head.

This is written from an oubliette deep in the Rock. We are to be ceremonially garrotted upstairs as an extra Tattoo treat on the Festival's closing night.

We retract nothing.

CHARLES REID

'*This isn't the way I imagined it.*'

108

Bertrand Russell and
the Infinite

"THE number of finite whole numbers must, therefore, be an infinite number. But now comes a curious fact: The number of even numbers must be the same as the number of all whole numbers. Consider the two rows:

$$1, \quad 2, \quad 3, \quad 4, \quad 5, \quad 6,\ldots$$
$$2, \quad 4, \quad 6, \quad 8, \quad 10, \quad 12,\ldots$$

There is one entry in the lower row for every one in the top row; therefore the number of terms in the two rows must be the same, although the lower row consists of only half the terms in the top row. Leibniz, who noticed this, thought it a contradiction . . . Georg Cantor, on the contrary, boldly denied that it is a contradiction. He was right; it is only an oddity.

"Georg Cantor defined an 'infinite' collection as one which has parts containing as many terms as the whole collection contains . . . thereby taking into the realm of exact logic a whole region formerly given over to mysticism and confusion."

LORD RUSSELL: *"History of Western Philosophy"*

LORD RUSSELL, from my earliest youth,
Inspired me with a zeal for Truth,
And oft when o'er his page I pored
I bowed my head and blessed the lord
For showing in so clear a light
The Nature of the Infinite
That even intellectual midgets
(Like me) could grasp it with their digits.
The method is, of course, to write 'em—
1, 2, 3, 4, *ad infinitum*
And then beneath each term affix
Its double, namely 2, 4, 6, . . .
The even and whole numbers thus
Are clearly equinumerous;
In brief, an Infinite Collection
Is equal to its own sub-section.

It thus becomes supremely plain
To any but the dimmest brain
Why "in all time" (Lord Russell's phrase)
There are as many years as days,
And also why a wise man sows
His cabbage-seed in finite rows.
(Those endless rows of Russell's sprout
As fast as one can thin them out.)

The Infinite, when once defined,
No longer stupefies the mind;
And though its properties appear,
Lord Russell says, a trifle queer,
He adds, in tones of deep conviction,
That they contain no contradiction,
And it is palpably absurd
For us to doubt Lord Russell's word.

E. V. MILNER

109

Down Among The Dinosaurs

In America one can sell anything—even dinosaur tracks. Recently I met a man who owns a dinosaur track quarry in Western Massachusetts, and sells his produce. The local gentry said I must meet Mr Nash, so I did. Up a dirt track near a village called South Hadley I found Dinosaurland—proprietor, Carlton S. Nash. There was a little souvenir shack and behind it a human track led up to the quarry. The quarry was shale, and Mr Nash has found tracks on every one of the sixteen layers he has already dug up. There were certainly tracks in the shale, three-toed affairs looking like petrified maple-leaves, which Mr Nash had polished up with linseed oil with the loving care one normally bestows only on an old cricket-bat.

Nash claims the abundance of tracks is due to the fact that this used to be an old dinosaur watering-hole. "Old" is something of that *rara avis*, an American understatement. Nash was pretty casual about the whole thing. "They're triassic. About one hundred and fifty million years old. I dig them up and sell them as Conversation Pieces for the fireplace

or patio." Unabashed by pre-history, he showed me his brochure entitled "Talking Petrified Footprints for Moderns," and explained that his selling motto was "For the man who has everything". The everything must include a few thousand dollars to spare to buy a set of big tracks. Of course one can buy a small individual track for about 12 dollars, but there is some doubt whether this is the track of a baby big dinosaur or an adult little dinosaur. It still makes a conversation piece according to Mr Nash.

I was a bit hazy about what he meant by conversation piece. I imagined everyone sitting out on a Californian patio sipping mint juleps. The host would say casually "Say, folks, have you seen my dinosaur tracks?" The guests would look up and say "Nope". The host would point to the tracks, carefully landscaped into his crazy-paving, and say "There it is". The more polite guests would say "Oh, are those real dinosaur tracks?" "Yep", the host would reply. Didn't seem much of a conversation to me. Of course there could be follow-ups like "Did it come with the house, or did you find it afterwards?" The host would be embarrassed into admitting that it was sent from Western Massachusetts wrapped in brown paper. The postman had staggered up the drive with it, and he had to pay 15 dollars postage. The postman had said "What you got in here—a body?" and he had replied "No, actually it's a footprint." "Must have been made by a goddam dinosaur," the postman said. He didn't want to seem a wise guy, so he said nothing.

This wasn't a conversation either; it was an anecdote. Still, Mr Nash seemed to be making a comfy living out of his conversation pieces, so obviously his patrons were more imaginative conversationally than I gave them credit for. Among his customers were Gene Autry, General and Mrs Patton, Dale Carnegie and Lowell Thomas. In fact in the brochure there is an extract from a letter from the Pattons' daughter—"Daddy and mother had always longed to have a set of tracks". Dale Carnegie wrote, "I want you to know how much I have enjoyed owning the Dinosaur prints. I prize them very highly. Every time I look at them I get a sense of perspective and of my own insignificance. My friends are pop-eyed when I show them footprints made by dinosaurs millions of years ago." And that from a man who knew how to make friends.

I left without buying a track, but I got to thinking about dinosaurs. Back in New York I went to the Museum of Natural History. I visited the Paleontology curator, an expert on dinosaurs and their tracks. He explained that there was nothing unusual in Nash finding tracks in the Connecticut River Valley of Western Massachusetts. They are more common up there than a four-leaf clover, and for Mr Nash much more profitable. The Valley is a triassic geological area, what is called Old Red Sandstone in Britain and found around Carlisle and Lossiemouth. The earliest dinosaurs were triassic and wandered around one hundred and fifty to two hundred million years ago, leaving their hefty footprints as conversation pieces for posterity. There are double profits to be made in the business too. One layer of rock contains the actual imprint, while the layer on top will contain a natural cast, and both can be sold.

A friend of the curator's arrived, and I was introduced. "This is Leonard Hungerford," said the curator, "he's an Australian concert pianist who collects dinosaur tracks. This is Mr Price who is interested in tracks." Mr Hungerford greeted me like a long-lost Christian brother in a heathen world. There seems to be a bond between dinosaur-track-collectors; they practically have a masonic handshake of their own. Mr Hungerford told me how he made some wonderful discoveries only fifty yards away from the Connecticut State Jail. He had begun digging and found a seam of large tracks, only to be arrested in mid-jubilation. The jail wardens had reported a suspicious figure trying to dig his way into the jail. The State Police arrived and offered him the courtesy of a formal question of intent: "What you doing, mister?" "I'm digging for dinosaur tracks, officer," Hungerford replied. That did it, and he was hauled off, protesting, to the police station. After a nightmarish session of explanation he was released, and the police helped him load the slab of tracks into his car. "I've had more publicity from finding those tracks than I've had from playing the piano round the world," Mr Hungerford complained. He invited me to see his collection at his home outside New York, a jumble of pre-history and music. My host flitted masterfully from the intricacies of a Brahms sonata to the imprints of Brontosaurus. It was a fascinating evening. As I left he pressed a two-foot slab of rock into my hand. "You must take this with you," he said. It was a perfect track of Cœlophysus. It was quite a conversation piece on the train home.

STANLEY PRICE

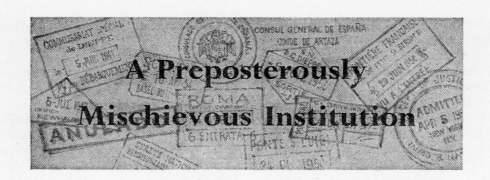
FEW of us can claim to have followed with passionate interest the activities of the Council of Europe Committee of Experts for the Simplification of Frontier Formalities (a body which, as an earnest of good faith, might set about simplifying its own name).

In its proposals to scrap the passport system the Committee has received little or no encouragement from the British Government. For once the Government is in touch with public opinion. It knows that most of us are so much in love with our passports that we would bitterly resent being ordered to throw them in the fire.

The old-fashioned notion that a passport was a badge of servitude and a ticket of leave we regard as the bemused vagary of a generation which stuffed itself with larks and lusted vainly after its deceased wife's sister.

To us, a passport is a fount of self-esteem. Smugly, we tot up the imprints of the Sûreté Nationale of Boulogne-sur-Mer and the Doorlaatpost at Venlo and reflect what restless cosmopolites we are. But items like those are only the chaff. Look at the splendid pages of Arabic and French, well worth the trouble of paying six visits to a sweaty police barracks in Ismailia. Look at the United States visa, with its whimsical memories of being finger-printed in Grosvenor Square and of a State Department so benevolent that it provided a well-equipped wash-room for no

other purpose than to remove ink from the digits of aliens.

For many of us, the saddest day is that on which our passport requires renewal, for it means abandoning a well-loved book full of exotic script and polyglot warnings, and starting off afresh with a couple of dozen virgin pages like any day tripper to Calais.

It has been said that our grandparents looked on the passport as something to be packed only if there was room, after the flea powder. The more headstrong of them chose to show their contempt for the system, and to add a meretricious zest to travel, by using somebody else's passport—a task made easier by the fact that the document was a mere square of folded paper, bearing no photograph. Others snorted around a visa-hungry Europe with no passport at all; their argument was that if you had no passport you were committing only one offence, whereas if you had a passport you were sure to be committing half a dozen. It is shocking, at this day, to think that Englishmen could have been guilty of such irresponsible casuistry.

Just a hundred years ago the subject of passports raised the national blood pressure to a dangerous level. There had been an attempt, in Paris, to assassinate the French Emperor. With irrefutable logic French officials argued that the way to prevent assassinations was to make all foreigners, even Englishmen, carry passports. (Even today those who admit to a desire to assassinate public officials are refused a visa to enter America, which shows that the French were on the right lines.)

At that time subjects of *Sa Majesté Britannique* resident in France were already under the necessity of obtaining passports from *Sa Majesté Très Chrétienne* of France (an unnecessary distinction there, as some thought). Henceforth, all Britons visiting France were required to possess passports, and not French passports but British ones. To obtain these they had to request mayors and magistrates to vouch for their probity. In those intolerant days mayors and magistrates were less inclined to rise from dinner tables or descend from stirrups in order to sign on dotted lines, so the circle of guarantors had to be widened to include professional men. Yet there were obstinate Englishmen who were not satisfied with this concession and who went about proclaiming loudly that they had always counted themselves fortunate in not knowing a lawyer or a surgeon.

bearings of the Foreign Minister? Surely the Englishman's honest face and vile accent were sufficient evidence of his identity?

It was not only in France that the more aggressive British travellers clashed with their hosts. On the frontiers of German pocket-states officials were roundly abused for presuming to scrutinize the lineaments of Englishmen and to compare them with the written tally. Some of these officials, it was thought, were rendered touchy by the ostentatious way in which the Foreign Minister of Great Britain introduced himself. Why should he think that, just because he was Warden of the Cinque Ports as well as a Privy Councillor, he could browbeat Reuss-Schleitz-Lobenstein? (It is significant that that sonorous catalogue of honours has recently been abandoned, probably as a belated concession to sensitive foreigners.)

No doubt, among the more apoplectic travellers, there were some who thought that their passports could have been worded, with advantage, on the lines of the safe-conduct issued by the Emperor

Today the priesthood of Printing House Square must blush to think how harshly their forbears berated the passport system, branding it as "the keystone in the gigantic arch of despotism which spans the Continent of Europe". Any Continental landlord, said *The Times*, would trust an Englishman for weeks and months, but he was now to be "a miserable unit in a police-ridden mob," a man in fetters, a dog with a tin kettle tied to his tail. Had not Lord Chesterfield said that a prepossessing appearance was the best letter of introduction? Why, then, should an Englishman rely for his safe-conduct on a piece of paper notable only for its sonorous catalogue of the names, titles, appointments and armorial

Augustus to Potamon the Philosopher: "If there be anyone on land or sea hardy enough to molest Potamon, let him consider whether he be strong enough to wage war with Cæsar."

The loyal French officials who pioneered the passport system were betrayed by their Emperor, who looked on their efforts with disfavour. Soon Englishmen were allowed to visit Calais and Boulogne without passports; by 1860 passports were no longer required for any part of France. As was to be expected, *The Times* hailed this lapse into anarchy with unseemly glee. "A thousand times," it said, "we have been assured that the abolition of the passport system was an impossibility . . . Six months hence both nations will be wondering why an institution so preposterously mischievous could ever have been maintained".

If *The Times* had been directed by men of vision it would have known that passports were bound to come back. Today the consensus of all responsible and tractable citizens the world over is that freedom to travel is, as they say in the Army, a privilege not a right. Now that it has had nearly a hundred years to reflect, let *The Times* inform the Council of Europe Committee of Experts for the Simplification of Frontier Formalities that the passport is part of the British heritage, a treasured possession not to be lightly discarded at the demand of preposterously mischievous agitators.

E. S. TURNER

After Reading You Know What

Just an extract from a quarter of a million words

18

THE walls of the room were covered with book-shelves. Each of these held many books. In one there was a little gap, like the gap in your comb when it begins to get old and broken.

In a chair in one corner of the room sat Ivan Alexandrovich Putthatin, an inspector of accidents from the Urals who had come to Moscow to live. He had begun to supplement his income by literary criticism. Sometimes on Sunday he would go for long bus-rides by himself, and one of his legs was shorter than the other.

The book he was reading was *Dr Zhivago*. It was this that had left the gap on one of the shelves. He read very slowly. At long intervals he turned a page, reading what was on the other side. The light was poor.

19

"But what is so noticeable is this continual alternation. I mean the alternation of concrete, pictorial detail with discussion. Heavens, what discussions!"

"What's wrong with them?"

"They go on and on. One speaker expounds a philosophical idea. It may be in two lines. It may be for half a page! With cries of discovery! The other replies, for half a page. And so on. But if you over-looked the quotation marks you would often think you were reading a somewhat inflated essay, by one person."

"These speeches are carefully considered. I'm sure they are full of meaning. But they have little to do with character. They demand more effort than I wish to make."

"I'm glad to hear you say that. If you hadn't, I should have said it myself. Good heavens! What are we arguing about?"

"We aren't arguing. We're agreeing. It's as you said a few moments ago."

"We are saying the same thing. But the reader has no way of telling which of us is which."

It was six months later. Ivan had finished the book. He had been paid for his review. The other speaker was a childhood friend of his named Olga

Andreyevna Droschky. He had met her by chance in the grocer's where he had gone to spend the money.

She had read the book too, rather more quickly. She skipped bits of the discussions. Her son's name was Kolya.

20

Some days later Ivan went for a bus-ride. It was not a Sunday. That would look too much like contrivance by the author. Everything must happen by accident. Ivan took the only remaining seat on the bus. It was next to a young man who wore his fur hat on one side, so that he looked like a broken candle.

The bus hummed along the road. After a time the young man spoke. He was beginning to grow a moustache.

"Have you read *Dr Zhivago?*"

"Yes. How extraordinary!"

"What is extraordinary?"

"That you should ask me about this book, which is in my mind constantly. Will you allow me to pay your fare?"

"As an employee of the bus company, I have a free pass. Thank you all the same."

This young man was none other than Kolya, son of Olga Andreyevna. He had recently left the university without taking his degree, and was now working as an assistant clerk.

Ivan saw a football-pitch covered with sheep, and got out of the bus. On one goal-post was a seagull.

21

Among the other passengers in the bus was Mikhail Konstantinovich Guvnor, a provincial librarian who had lost all his books in the hurricane of 1922. Since then, he had been keeping an inn in the Urals. Ivan had once inspected one of his accidents. When the bus reached the terminus he got out and began to walk back. His felt boots crackled on the dusty road.

After walking for several hours he met Ivan. He had known this would happen.

"The name for it is *chosisme*, isn't it?"

"Perhaps. But I think that is a word of later origin."

"Nevertheless on page 91 we find the word 'psychiatrist'. Was that word known in 1911?"

"I don't suppose it was. Why do you ask?"

"I should like your copy of the book to start my library again. I have come to the conclusion that

'*You're not really being much help, are you?*'

115

there is no future in innkeeping. Will you give it to me?"

"Willingly. How strange that you should ask! I had already wrapped it in newspaper, fearing rats."

"You seem to take a gloomy view."

"I am an inspector of accidents."

"Of course! I had forgotten."

They walked together along the road towards Moscow. From time to time they met people they had not seen for many years, and recalled childhood memories. This delayed their progress. It grew dark.

22

Mikhail Konstantinovich followed Ivan into his room. The gap in the shelf had been filled with another book. Ivan went at once to a table in the corner.

"How stupid of me to forget! I gave it away."

"It's of no consequence. Goodbye. I expect we shall meet again."

"That is almost certain."

The street watched the room through the window. Several streets in *Dr Zhivago* do this. They don't see very much.

RICHARD MALLETT

Dip. Imm.

I CROSSED the threshold clutching my infant son (eight months, nineteen pounds, two teeth) and the postcard requesting his 10 a.m. attendance for Dip. Imm. The waiting room was bright above with posters showing How To Catch A Cold, and dark below with struggling mothers, acrobatic babies, adventurous toddlers, and schoolchildren demented with exuberance at missing Maths. and Geog. Sound effects included the *Titanic* going down and Destry doing encores.

"Bit of a crush," said the mum in front of me. "But you get used to it. He's my fifth." She tipped her head towards a grubby little boy engaged in stealing a jet plane from a nearby shopping-bag.

I smiled uncertainly enough to be taken under her wing. "You just queue up here, see, and give your card in at the window. After a bit they call your name." Suddenly she turned away and I heard a stinging slap.

"Ronald, I *told* you if I had to tell you again . . ."

A boy called Charles was lying on my feet in spite of instructions from his mother to the contrary. I felt the tickle of a nylon ladder rushing from his space-gun to my knee.

We reached the window, where there was a dear, white-coated lady serene enough to be stone deaf. She flipped along a row of cards, selected one, and told me to sit down.

But where? Perhaps on the floor. One mother was already there, her flung arm clutching at a sandalled foot protruding from the space beneath the Dried Milk cupboard.

There were comics everywhere. The squeaky toys were squeaking, the invisible machine-guns stuttering, the fruity lollies melting.

"'Ere y'are, love!" cried a voice. "Ernie, stand up and let the lady sit down." I subsided gratefully on to a ravaged packet of potato crisps.

At 10 a.m. a nurse appeared. We saw her lips churn out the shapes of names, but we heard nothing. Nothing, that is, except the Destry-*Titanic* saga, spiced up now with the crash and scream of a child inside a case of orange-juice empties.

Then suddenly there was an almost-hush, ripped only by shushing and giggles. Names were called, and Dawns and Marlenes swished their pony-tails towards the surgery, followed by Peters and Davids pulling up their socks and wrapping sodden blobs of chewing-gum in their hankies.

Confusion burst again with much demand for penny-spending. Two big girls clutched each other's shoulders and confessed they daren't go in, honest they daren't.

At last our turn came round. A dab of reeking cotton-wool, a prick, a whimper, and the deed was done. I spilled my infant back into his pram where he immediately assumed the shape of a treble clef. I was still unravelling him when Ronald and his mum appeared. From Ronald's blazer pocket peeped the grey nose of a jet plane.

"I'll never get dipferia now, will I, mum?" he crowed.

The jet plane soared into the air between his mother's fingers. "Here's something you *will* get," she said, delivering a crippling blow at Ronald's starboard wing.

HAZEL TOWNSON

'*I feel awful.*'

'No, no, the milk comes out here.'

Sex

WITHOUT a Sextant sailors are at sea.
   Sextet sounds more refined than half a dozen,
And this year marks the Sexcentenary
   Of John of Gaunt's first marriage (to his cousin).

Sextillions signify extreme plurality.
   Sext is an office, mainly monasterial.
Sexisyllabic is unpunctuality.
   Sexpartite is a television serial.

Sexagenarians seek Retirement Pensions.
   Lent steels the Will ten days from Sexagesima,
Though steel production was of small dimensions
   Until Sextupled by Sir Henry Bessemer.

A Sextary is briefly undefinable.
   Sexfoiled, though unrepressed, are flowers (see Botany).
Sex is a Latin number, indeclinable;
   To go on further would be sheer monotony.

E. V. MILNER

DOUANES

Alex Atkinson's

A Short Guide to British Politics

1. The Tories

ALTHOUGH it may seem to some people that the Conservatives have always been with us, sitting in their clubs with newspapers over their heads, complaining about the price of Stilton and the noise of these new-fangled horseless omnibuses, the incredible fact is that for hundreds of years the country somehow managed to get along fairly well *without* them. Granted, it was a pretty shiftless sort of existence, with no proper system of stocks and shares, hardly any drains, and no Australia to play cricket against: all the same, we muddled along without a single Young Conservative to stand up boldly and tell us who was ready for self-government and who was not, whose son should go to Eton and whose son should not, and what to do about the Middle East. It wasn't until the reign of Charles I that Conservatism showed any signs of sprouting, but as we look back we must acknowledge that its emergence was inevitable. I don't know whether it's the Gulf Stream, or our habit of eating roast beef and two veg. or what, but one can no more imagine Britain without Conservatives than Tibet without the Yak or Grunting Ox.

At first they weren't called Conservatives, and their early history is confused, to say the very least. Evidently some wise man rose one day and said "Look here, steady on, chaps. The country's going from bad to worse, what with everyone rushing about discovering places, and inventing things, and asking questions, and generally getting things done. What we need is a sprinkling of responsible men to find some kind of status quo, and preserve it." These men were found—spry little chaps with striped trousers, twinkling eyes and drooping moustaches, who could talk like Dutch uncles and take tea with the nobility without turning a hair. They hunted around until they found what looked like a status quo, and they've been keeping it ever since, against all comers, in a little box marked "Pending". (They took it out now and then, to dust it, and were sometimes surprised to find that it had changed, all by itself, in the dark. One day, for instance, it might involve the sending of small boys up chimneys; another day it might require the closing of the Suez Canal. It is, in fact a source of constant wonder to its guardians, who secretly wish it was even half as rigid as the hidebound dogma of the Socialists.)

Now these men were called Tories, which turns out to be an Irish word, as if the whole business weren't complicated enough already. During some wars in Ireland in the reign of Elizabeth I, Tories were robbers who went about preying on Englishmen and Spaniards indiscriminately. These ruffians were particularly prominent during the Protestant massacres of 1641. When, therefore, a body of Englishmen in 1680 poured scorn on the Popish Plot while at the same time encouraging the Papists to revive it, because they wanted to banish the Duke of Monmouth and bring back the Duke of York, it was quite natural that they should come to be called "Tories" —or at any rate it seemed a good joke at the time; and the name stuck until 1833, when a man named Croker, writing in the *Quarterly Review*, wittily suggested that "Conservatives" would be more appropriate, since what they were after was to maintain existing conditions, which were horrible. That name has stuck ever since. The one thing that all Conservatives are thankful for, apart from the foresight of their leader in wearing a droll hat for his visit to Moscow, is that they are not still called Abhorrers. This name was fastened on them during the fuss about the Duke of Monmouth, when they tried to stop the Bill of Exclusion on the ground that they abhorred it. They are still inclined to abhor things, occasionally even throwing up their hands in horror and crying "Shame!" or "Withdraw!" but the name has never been really popular. After all, practically *anyone* can pronounce "Conservatism".

For the best part of the eighteenth century they had to sit in opposition, the government being in the hands of some extraordinary people called Whigs, owing to the whim of the Hanoverian sovereigns, who found still another name for the Tories, which was "Jacobites". This period was most distasteful to the Tories: they have never been at their best in opposition, because their chief parliamentary strength lies in finding excuses, turning away wrath, disguising unpopular measures as genuine boons, and passing

'*Then we had le coq au vin de Bourgogne, accompanied by a Chambolle Musigny,* 1940.'

in a lordly way revolutionary bills which their left-wing opponents have been trying to screw up enough courage to suggest for years. During the American war they distinguished themselves by insisting that the colonies should stay in the Empire, which would certainly have made the preparations for summit conferences a little less prolonged, if nothing else. Later, the party split hopelessly on the question of the repeal of the Corn Laws, which were giving ammunition to a couple of Manchester hotheads called Cobden and Bright. Disraeli, abhorring the repeal, led the Young England party from which sprang the Conservative party as we know it, and it seems likely to be with us for a very long time. Disraeli, a fancy dresser with a rich wife and a string of novels to his name, laid down the aims of the party as "the preservation of our institutions, the maintenance of our Empire, and the amelioration of the condition of the people". He looked more like George Arliss than anyone before or since, and he was one of the few people who knew how to handle Queen Victoria.

In foreign policy the Conservatives took as their slogan "Peace With Honour," which appears to have pleased everybody until the appeasement of the Nazis set in. During that period—and indeed ever since the Campbell-Bannerman administration—one of the liveliest opponents of the Conservatives was Winston Churchill, a dashing figure who had served with the Spanish forces in Cuba during the Spanish-American war, sat for Oldham as a Conservative and N.W. Manchester as a Liberal, and campaigned vigorously against the militant suffragettes, who threw things at him. In 1940, with far-reaching consequences, he became Prime Minister, and the Conservatives claimed him as their own. But even he could not win them the 1945 election, when they came out gaily for unfettered enterprise and the abolition of control and the Labour Party, to its considerable astonishment, awoke to find itself a power in the land. But the Conservatives are nothing if not resilient; it wasn't long before they were back in favour, sending troops to Egypt as to the manner born, and smiling upon the Welfare State as though they had recently hatched it. Today, it may be said that the Conservatives are Right-wing Socialists, just as the Socialists are Left-wing Conservatives, and it is getting more and more difficult to work up any really genuine row in the House. The status quo has been taken out of its box, and may be seen riotously changing shape and colour almost from day to day. It has finally been decided, after a couple of hundred years or so, that a status quo is easier to preserve that way.

As to the Conservatives, Jacobites, Abhorrers or Tories themselves, many of them are barely recognizable. They are poorer, for one thing, except the poor ones, who are richer. They still don't talk much on trains, but they tend to have a little more respect for what used to be called the working classes, who may be able to give them a lift to the station one of these days, what with all this free enterprise, and you can't be too careful. They are more daring about food and furniture than they used to be. They are even beginning to take an interest in politics. They are still suspicious of Picasso, Ibsen, Stravinsky, Tom Paine, W. C. Handy, and others of the *avant garde*. They are justly proud of the fact (although it still frightens them a bit to think how daring they were) that it was they who gave pensions to widows and orphans, not to mention old-age pensions to insured men and wives at sixty-five. When they have properly adjusted themselves to the fact that the Centre has moved well over to the Left, there seems to be no reason why they shouldn't find their balance, sit firmly in the saddle and carry on, in their imperturbable fashion, just as though nothing had happened.

2. The Socialists

THE Labour Party was formed, more in hope than in anger, in 1900, and gave rise almost immediately to one J. Ramsay MacDonald, whose moustache was to be bread-and-butter to cartoonists for a decade, and who reached his highest peak of happiness on the morning when every duchess in London wanted to kiss him, for reasons best known to himself. The party seems to have been invented by amalgamating the I.L.P., a sinister-looking bunch of malcontents commonly supposed to carry bombs in their overcoat pockets, with the Fabian Society, a group of vegetarians with hairy clothes, who believed in John Stuart Mill, Bernard Shaw, and something called the inevitability of gradualness. The Fabians were apt to sit about writing tracts and pamphlets on such outlandish subjects as unemployment, which until then had been regarded as a cross between an act of God and sheer bone idleness.

The movement has never really found favour among people who stick out their little finger when drinking tea, and the chief reason for this is that one of its begetters was an Ayrshire man called Keir Hardie, who never went to school in his life and was uncouth enough to go and work in a pit, of all places, at the age of ten. As one of the first Labour M.P.s he greatly amused the smart set by wearing a cloth cap in Westminster and getting himself worked up about people who didn't appear to have much background, let alone shoes or stockings. As a matter of fact, right down to the present day the Labour party has kept on throwing the most frightfully bizarre or undesirable-looking characters in the face of the public, dammit. MacDonald himself came from a tumbledown shack in some unfashionable place called Lossiemouth, and never uttered a sentence that contained less than a thousand words, most of which were rhetorical, not to say downright interchangeable. To balance this there was Clement Attlee, a public school man who was about as garrulous as Gary Cooper, only not so tall. In between there came such obviously impossible people as Mrs Braddock, who knew swear-words and interviewed callers while ironing shirts in the sitting-room, and Aneurin Bevan, who was caddish enough to remember unpleasant things about coal-mines, and suggested publicly that there were a number of underprivileged people in Britain, although he took care not to name any of them specifically.

The party was unpopular on all sides at the outset. The idea that a lot of uninformed clods should come shambling into the House of Commons, misplacing their aspirates and openly talking about slums was most distasteful to the great majority of English people. By a tradition that went back as far as Aristotle it had been generally accepted that politics should be quietly managed by gentlemen

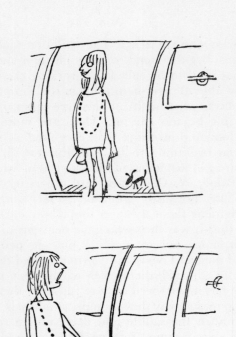

who bought their shirts by the dozen, knew a good claret when they smelt one, and always had a choice of three house-parties for Goodwood. Even the working-classes (who were at that time well on the way to becoming a distinct species, even having their own separate diseases) threw up their hands in horror when these newfangled Labour people tried to persuade them that they were down-trodden wage-slaves being exploited by cynical capitalists on the one hand and degenerate landed gentry on the other.

For many years, therefore, the Labour Party had to devote a good deal of time and energy to getting the proletariat accustomed to the ideas of Robert Owen, Rousseau and Saint-Simon, not to mention Marx and Engels. It was an uphill task. Many an unemployed labourer in 1912, living with his wife and six children in one rat-haunted room, would no more dream of casting a vote for Labour than he would omit to touch his hat and simper whenever he saw his landlord. Right up to the nineteen-twenties it took a bold man to admit that he had thrown in his lot with the raggle-taggle Socialists, who seldom shaved, and were always complaining, and made the public bar smell so, and probably wanted to blow up Buckingham Palace, and went on hunger marches in such awful clothes, and had thoughts above their station, and fell down drunk in the streets, and so far demeaned themselves as to ask for bread, and actually maintained that a lad who learned his sums at a village school and then became a cowman had as much right to piped water and a holiday with pay as the son of a lord who would never do a hand's turn even when he had inherited ten acres of desirable London property at the age of twenty-one.

Gradually, however, and chiefly through the support of the trade union and co-operative movements, the down-trodden masses were made to admit that the dice *might* be loaded just a fraction in favour of the bloated capitalists (who were, as a matter of strict historical **accuracy**, usually inclined to be on the gaunt side, and troubled with dypsepsia). At last, in 1924, Labour had the audacity to win an election and almost before anyone knew what was happening they put through a Housing Act, a Minimum Agricultural Wages Act, and a measure to increase the range of old-age pensions. This might seem revolutionary enough, but it didn't satisfy the I.L.P. members. They pig-headedly continued to demand "Socialism in our time" and set up a left wing opposition within the party. The precise meaning of "Socialism in our time" has never been

'Sheer physical exhaustion—lay off action painting for the time being.'

satisfactorily established. Thus, to some it might mean Nationalization of Everything Overnight, while to others it might mean the rattle of the tumbril in Pall Mall, the setting up of barricades, the looting of the Athenaeum, and the crowning of Mr Cousins on the steps of Transport House. Whatever its significance the split has never quite healed, and today the party is at great pains to deny that it exists, the denials growing the more vociferous the more dangerously it yawns.

During the nineteen-thirties a lot of people called intellectuals came crowding into the party. On account of their greasy sweaters and burning, deep-set eyes some of them were suspected of being Communist infiltrators, although they swore they were simply Tolstoyan liberals from the London School of Economics. Ever since then the membership of the party has been changing, until today it would be quite wrong to assume that the shabby out-of-work at the dogs is the only one who clings to

Socialism as the answer to man's dreams. He has been joined by the free-thinking young scientist in the Chelsea maisonette, coming down to breakfast in his sandals and finishing the *Listener* crossword in twenty minutes flat by the cuckoo clock his mistress brought back from Austria.

Labour people today tend to use long words, know a lot about politics, complain that the *New Statesman* is not as good as it was, fasten their neckties loosely, prefer old cars and undubbed Continental films, have a lively contempt for Annigoni and Wilson Steer, wish they *really* liked the *Mirror*, and pretend they know just what Mr Gaitskell means when he talks of "planned economy". If anything they are rather more set in their ways than the Conservatives. They have never forgiven Edward VII for saying "We are all Socialists nowadays," and today, as they sit in opposition and see so many of their ideas being put into practice almost as a matter of course, they are apt to wonder just who *won* the revolution.

3. The Liberals

THE Liberal Party, which believes in liberty, is the party of the future. It has been the party of the future for quite some time now. Before that it was for many years the party of the past, and very little was heard about it: it seemed to have vanished after the Great War, leaving only a faint smell of Free Trade behind it. It now appears, however, that ever since that time mysterious underground forces have been ceaselessly toiling to restore it to its former power and glory, so that at any moment we are likely to be faced with a triumphant resurgence, in which soberly clad crowds will fill the streets, marching steadily on the capital with banners, being courteous to the mounted police and bravely chanting "Peace, entrenchment and reform!" Secret printing presses have been humming day and night, turning out pamphlets, policy statements, battle plans and photographs of Lady Violet Bonham Carter, all equally mysterious. Quietly spoken men in pubs have spread a strange, intangible doctrine, pouring subtle scorn alike on Socialist and Tory. Never put into humdrum words, but conveyed rather by meaning nods and winks, a loftily confident sip at a medium sherry, or the use of beguiling slabs of mumbo-jumbo such as "abrogation of speculative foundations and reliance on social utility," the doctrine has delicately settled over the whole population like a vast, tenuous but inescapable cobweb. Labour and Conservative alike, men in marginal constituencies lie awake at night trying to fathom what it might be, and whence it might come, and whether it might save them and their helpless, trusting families from the harsh, bleak anxieties of living. "Is this," they ask themselves, sitting up in bed and switching on the light, like primitive man aroused in his cave by the first stirrings of social conscience, or the dread snakes, or a nagging urge to construct a round flat stone thing with a hole in the centre to take an axle—"is this the Answer I have sought in vain so long? And will it work? And what the devil *is* it?"

What it is is Liberalism, and what that is, even in a world where everyone from Khrushchev to Salazar boldly claims to have a liberal outlook, is anybody's guess. Toryism and Socialism are relatively simple: the one means succour and protection for the down-trodden shareholders quietly starving in their four-door family saloons, hardly knowing where the next expense-account is coming from; the other means control by the humble striker of the means of production, distribution and exchange, not to mention the abolition of all private property except the humble strikers'. These are obviously both fine, deserving causes, and no Englishman worth his salt could refrain from throwing his hat in the air and cheering for one or the other of them—or even both, if he wanted to be on the safe side. But with Liberalism we seem to enter the realms of fantasy, a place where Englishmen have always felt uncomfortable and suspicious. Ask the man in the street to march to the House of Commons shouting "Down with flipping landlords!" or "Hands off the Steel Industry if you don't mind!" or any similarly clarion call, and he will be with you like a shot, with a flask of tea in his haversack and a plastic mac in case it rains. Suggest, on the other hand, that he should carry a banner bearing the demand *Such Government By The People As Will Maintain Individual Liberty To The Maximum Extent Compatible With Social Order*, and he will shuffle away nervously blushing.

In order to see the beginnings of Liberalism it is necessary to take a quick look back into history; and even that won't help. Up to the time of Gladstone (a Liberal), for as long as anyone could remember there had been people called Whigs. Little is known of them either, but to hear him on the subject one would think they had been got together for the express purpose of annoying Dr Johnson (a Tory).

It was Johnson's opinion that the first Whig was the Devil, but this has never been satisfactorily proved. To complicate the issue farther Labouchère (a journalist, and a Liberal to boot) said he didn't object to Gladstone's always having the ace of trumps up his sleeve, but only to his pretence that God had put it there. Actually the Whigs began as a kind of secret society in the time of Charles II (an Independent), and eventually emerged as a party opposed to the power of the monarch and in favour of rule by Parliament and the people. It turned out that what they meant by the people was the upper classes. But after the passing of the Reform Bill in 1832 the Whigs turned into Liberals and proceeded to madden the Tories by insisting that all kinds of extraordinary people should have the right to vote, such as grown men and women. This threw everything into confusion. English history became a battle between Gladstone and Disraeli (a Tory), and it would take a brave man to say who won. There now follow some notable dates:

1886 Liberal Unionists, opposing Gladstone's Home Rule policy, joined the Tories.
1894 Lord Rosebery's horse (a Liberal) won the Derby.
1895 Same again.
1896 Lloyd George (a Liberal) suspended from Lord Salisbury's government for obstruction.
1901 Lloyd George disguised as a policeman in Birmingham.
1905 Lord Rosebery's horse won the Derby.

After the Great War it was generally assumed that

'How's that for sales resistance?'

quite enough had been done for liberty for the time being, and the Liberals withdrew from the arena, evidently deciding to bide their time until the invention of television. Now, at last they are on the march again.

I have not myself been invited to play any prominent part in the current resuscitation of Liberalism. If I *am* asked, however, I shall have my answer ready. "In view," I shall say, "of the fact that those horses of Lord Rosebery's kept on winning the Derby, it strikes me as little short of odd that there should be no racing page in the *Manchester Guardian*. How can I be expected," I shall ask, "to strike a blow for liberty, which your Mr Asquith defined as 'the right, so long as a man did not become a danger or a nuisance to the community, to use as he thought best the faculties of his nature, or his brains, and the opportunities of his life', if I am to be deprived of the probable runners and riders at Bogside, Chepstow, Newmarket or San-

down Park?" They will thereupon remind me, in those calm, unruffled Liberal tones, of Professor Hobhouse's observation to the effect that the Liberal movement has often sought to dispense with general principles, which explains its frequent inconsistencies.

Finally, my investigations lead me to the intriguing conclusion that as things stand at present ninety per cent of Englishmen are Liberals at heart. "Mind you," they will say, having been forced into an untenable position in defence of either Toryism or Socialism, "I suppose I'm really a Liberal, if the truth were known". This is due partly to the English love of compromise (for there is a widely held theory that Liberalism is a kind of genial cross between Socialism and Conservatism), and partly to the fascination of the unknown. At all events, Liberalism certainly seems due for another run, and I hope I may still be alive when the great day comes. Otherwise I don't see how I'm ever going to discover what it's all about.

'Why, Mrs Norris, I didn't know your son was musical.'

Happy Wanderers

WE have sat on foreign stations in the middle of the night
  Doing little sums of currency on greasy paper-bags.
We have stumbled half-exhausted up a seventh pension flight
  To a doubtful, itchy mattress that unquestionably sags.

We have travelled third and thirsty over weary miles of plain
  With a loaf and half a sausage for our breakfast, lunch and dinner.
We have frittered hours at frontiers and been frisked inside the train,
  And departed from the Customs looking noticeably thinner.

We have stayed where no one goes to bed and everybody sings
  To the clattering accompaniment of cobbles under clogs.
We have lost our luggage, temper, way, and many other things;
  We have sacrificed our bacon; we have even eaten frogs.

And the funny thing about it is the way we swagger home
  With our pottery, embroidery and basket-work and views,
Telling lies about the weather and the grandeur that was Rome;
  Feeling *sorry* for the Joneses in a houseboat on the Ouse.

HAZEL TOWNSON

America Day by Day

P. G. Wodehouse reporting

AUSTERE theatregoers who hold that musical comedy should be a grim and smileless thing, purging the soul with pity and terror, received a shock the other day when a tuneful trifle called *Say, Darling*, without a single death scene in it, opened on Fifty-Second Street and not only opened but stayed open. Being the hero of a modern musical has come to be ranked as one of the dangerous trades, but the principal character in this one gets through to the final curtain without so much as a flesh wound, How different from the home life of the juvenile lead in such a divertissement as *West Side Story*. It is a revolutionary departure but one which, however disappointing to the undertakers in the audience, has the support of the general public.

Say, Darling is by Richard Bissell, who wrote the novel which was made into the musical *The Pajama Game*. He then wrote a novel describing his experiences as a novelist whose novel is made into a musical, and this novel has been made into the musical *Say, Darling*. He is reported to be working on a novel about a novelist who has his novel made into a musical and writes a novel about a novelist who has his novel made into a musical, and where it will all end, knows God, as *Time* would say. I am watching the situation very closely.

* * *

Dieting continues to be all the go on this side of the Atlantic, and the number of those who push their plates away untasted increases daily. But there are still some sturdy souls who enjoy a square meal, notably in Detroit, Michigan. Dr Joseph Molner, the Health Commissioner of that city, has recently published a list of the peculiar things eaten and drunk by the citizens during his three years of office. It includes insecticides, detergents, laundry bleaches, shoe-polish, glue, chalk and charcoal, washed down with ink, hair-setting lotion and lighter fluid. I have never actually attended any of these Detroit parties, but the picture I conjure up is of a sort of Dickens Christmas, the detergent bowl circulating freely and the air ringing with merry cries of "Don't spare the shoe-polish, Percy," and "After you with the insecticide, George". And the extraordinary thing is that the revellers seem to thrive on the stuff. The rosy cheeks and sparkling eyes to be seen in Detroit would reach, if placed end to end, for miles and miles and miles.

* * *

I was speaking not long ago of the remarkable improvement in American manners, at one time inclined to be brusque, and eulogizing the new spirit of considerateness which you see on every side nowadays. A striking example of this spirit was given in Milwaukee recently, when Paul Chaney (26) appeared in the District Court, charged with having thrown a large brick through the bedroom window of a girl friend with whom he had had a tiff of some nature. Asked why he had done this, he replied: "I threw the brick through the bedroom window because I didn't want to disturb anyone else in the house."

No doubt he had asked himself what the Chevalier Bayard would have done, and this was it.

Amiable Volatiles

Peter Dickinson

On September 2, 1870, M. la Perre de Roo read in *The Times* that Paris, where he was then living, was about to be invested by the Germans; so he immediately wrote to the Minister of War suggesting that all the pigeons in Paris should be commandeered and sent to the country and that all the pigeons at Lille and Roubaix should be brought to Paris. Unfortunately the government fell next day and the letter was lost; when the President of the Société Colombophile l'Espérance went to the new Minister of War to offer the services of the birds of his society he was only able to interview a lieutenant who laughed in his face, with the Prussians at the gates of Paris. Soon all communication with the rest of France was cut off.

At this point M. Rampont, the Postmaster-General, had the luminous conception that it might be possible to communicate by balloon, and on September 23 at eight in the morning the balloon *Neptune*, commanded by the aeronaut Duruof, rose from Montmartre to the frenetic applause of the besieged populace. But by evening gloom and discouragement succeeded; they had watched the balloon out of sight; they could hope it had safely traversed the enemy lines; but they knew nothing.

The same evening M. Louis van Rosebeke, Vice-President of the Société Colombophile l'Espérance, resolved the problem. What easier than to ferry racing pigeons out of Paris by balloon? On landfall the aeronaut could in a trice scribble a message and entrust it to a bird which would soon be winging homeward to its familiar loft. On September 25 the balloon *La Ville de Florence*, commanded by the aeronaut G. Mangin, left Paris carrying several sacks of dispatches and M. van Rosebeke's three best birds. By nightfall all three were home with messages reporting the safe arrival of the balloon at Triel. Such a colombophile triumph could not pass unremarked; as M. la Perre de Roo says, *grâce à ces aimables volatiles Paris avait cessé d'être isolé.*

Next a pigeon returned to announce the safe descent of M. Godard's double balloon *Les Etats-Unis;* on the morrow *Le Céleste* commanded by

IT is always sad when a man sees a great future for his own particular interest, when world-wide attention has been aroused by some event in which it played an indispensable part, when the letters of inquiry and offers of capital are pouring in by every post, and then an easier way of performing the same service is suddenly discovered. That is what happened to M. la Perre de Roo and his racing pigeons. Most of my information on the events that led up to his disappointment comes from his monograph on the care of those birds, and, his style being curiously pervasive, so does much of my syntax:

'When you've quite finished with your imitations.'

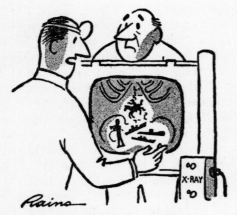

'I'm taking you off cornflakes!'

M. Tissandier, author of *En Ballon pendant le Siège de Paris*, left with three pigeons, several sacks of dispatches and a thousand proclamations to scatter on the heads of the Prussians, and by eight o'clock two pigeons were back with the news that he was safely down at Dreux; another reported the arrival of *L'Armand-Barbès* at Montdidier.

But then began a series of colombophile disasters, with valuable pigeons lost by being released in a contrary wind, in mist, rain or fog, or at nightfall, and by inexperienced men used to nothing but the management of a balloon. The solution was not to be ignored, and of the several members of the Société l'Espérance who left by ensuing balloons most arrived safely, though M. van Rosebeke suffered a broken ankle and only his presence of mind saved his birds after his aeronaut had fallen out of the *nacelle* when trying to land his balloon at night in a high wind.

Hitherto the pigeons had been able to report little but the safe arrival of the balloons, but on November 12 the balloon *Niepce* left with M. Dagron, the famous photographer, M. Fernique, the engineer, two of M. Dagron's assistants and 600 kilos of photographic equipment. M. Dagron was to try to set up a photomicrographic service and M. Fernique to experiment with a system of underwater communication along the Seine. The *Daguerre* was launched at the same time, and the two balloons drifted off together. As they passed over the Prussian lines both were assailed with volleys of rifle fire, and the passengers in the *Niepce* observed that the *Daguerre* was hit; horrified they watched its vertiginous descent on to the wall of a farm, where the Uhlans galloped up and captured it. The *Niepce* floated on unharmed but, being heavily laden, was forced to make its landfall dangerously close to Paris. At once it was surrounded by a crowd of countryfolk, who hastened to clothe the balloonists in peasant caps and blouses; two carts were brought and the equipment loaded on to them, but before they could be set in motion the Prussians arrived, seized one of the carts and lined up the assembled peasants, among whom were the balloonists. Fortunately the disguises were convincing and not a shot was fired. Then the Prussians became so deeply engaged in capturing the balloon that the passengers were able to escape with the second cart and make their way to the house of the local *curé;* he had Prussians billeted on him, so passed his visitors on to a colleague over the hill. By such surreptitious routes the party eventually made their way to Tours. There, thanks to M. Dagron's mastery of the photomicrographic tech-

nique, whereby a single bird could carry up to fifty thousand dispatches, an adequate pigeon postal service was established.

Very soon a working routine was in being. Each day M. Dagron would photograph the necessary dispatches, and next morning MM. Cassiers, van Rosebeke, Traclet, and Thomas would release the pigeons. Forty-four times during the siege these devoted men advanced almost to the lines of the Prussians to liberate their birds. At daybreak, when the fields were empty, when there was no one to be seen upon the roads but enemies, when no railway engine any more used the tracks across the abandoned countryside, a single locomotive, expressly heated for these brave colombophiles, sped with a single closed truck along rust-eaten rails towards the enemy lines. There they released their pigeons and the engine went as quickly as possible into reverse in order to return these gallant delegates of the Postal Service to their starting point.

Then Paris capitulated. But its agony had not, from the point of view of the Société l'Espérance, been wholly in vain. Now surely the world would have to

take them seriously; no more could lieutenants laugh in the face of the President. Pigeons were the coming thing.

M. la Perre de Roo was much occupied with the future of the pigeon, designing a military dove-house and a special wagon for use in the field; he was consulted by nine European governments on the subject, devised a method whereby the Portuguese customs could capture smugglers, and advised Trinity House on the use of pigeons in lightships. In vain, or nearly in vain. Within five years, during a breakdown of the cable between the Isle of Wight and the British mainland, the Post Office was able to communicate by means of wireless telegraphy. It is true that during the 1914-18 war the first air-sea rescue operation would have been a failure had not a messenger pigeon dropped dead in Yarmouth; true too that there was still a War Office establishment for pigeons during the more recent holocaust. But it must have been a small affair, no barracks, no bomb-proof pigeon-lofts, no brigadiers. Perhaps only a lieutenant, keen but long inured to being laughed in the face.

India is Not What it Was

INDIANS don't sit on spikes any more. Spikes seem to have gone out of fashion in India since Independence. Even the billion-pound Tata steelworks have turned their attention to the manufacture of other more easily saleable goods: rails, girders, steel plates.

Mr Nehru is largely responsible for these new trends in fashion. He is modernizing the country at an incredible pace. The very first day he became Prime Minister of India he arrived at the P.M.'s Secretariat in a high-powered limousine instead of a bullock cart. Because it was an American car from the old Viceregal garage he decreed that there should be no strings attached. He has to use British and American cars because the Russians have not yet presented him with a Rabblewaggon. In fact they have not given him anything very much except a private plane and the blue-prints of a collective farm.

Spikes, they say, used to help the Indians to think. Thought needs concentration. In the days of the old British raj, spikes provided stimulation. Nowadays the Indians have become much too thick-skinned and spikes don't work. It used to be all right when India's political philosophy was based on passive resistance. Now there is a new dynamic approach, a different outlook. You cannot fulfil a Five Year Plan on a five-point spike. Mr Nehru has, therefore, rightly cut spikes out.

Now that is not the only misconception which people in Britain have about India. In South Kensington the other day an intelligent English-woman asked me if I did the rope-trick. She said she did not believe it could be done, and if I said I could do it, would I show her.

I said "Madam, Indians don't have to do the rope-trick any more".

I explained that the idea of the rope-trick was purely a figment of British imperialist imagination. It was a sort of challenge to the Indian—an unfair challenge. If the poor bloke could not do it he would feel he had an inferiority complex, which was exactly what the British wanted.

But nowadays there is no need for the Indian to prove he is equal. He is every bit as good as the American, the British, the French and even the Egyptian. At the United Nations Mr Krishna Menon has talked out Sir Pierson Dixon many a time. So why do we have to prove our mettle by doing the rope-trick? The South Kensington lady understood.

Now there is another misconception—that all Indians are always hungry. In the days of the old raj the British deliberately kept the Indians on low-caloried diets. It was based on the mistaken belief that low calories produced low passive resistance.

The Indian national leaders soon put this right. Each time Mr Nehru spoke on Chowpatty sands in Bombay a hundred thousand hungry Indians were charged with patriotism. Now that the British have gone we have no more food problems. We can easily borrow from abroad.

Mr Mikoyan

MIHAIL MIKOYAN
Appears to be the doyen
Of that obsequious clique of Reds
Who've kept not only office but their heads.

NICOLAS BENTLEY

133

There have been other experiments tried to make ourselves self-sufficient in food. We tried out Japanese ways of rice cultivation, Australian dairy methods, Soviet systems of procurement, marketing and distribution; but in the end we have found it easier to borrow from Canada and the U.S., and it helps out with their over-production problems.

There is also a misconception that there is prohibition in India. Admittedly there are irksome liquor laws in some States of the Indian Union, but, as in all cases of regimentation, man and nature contrive to find a way out.

According to these liquor laws a foreigner (to India) is entitled to four units. He gets a permit to that effect on presentation of his passport. When he goes into a licensed bar he produces his permit, calls for a scotch-and-soda and gets it duly chalked up on his permit—$\frac{1}{27}$ of a unit gone. Balance: $3\frac{26}{27}$ units left. This balance is entered on the permit by the barman, countersigned by the hotel accountant on behalf of the licencee under the supervision of the Excise inspector on the spot, who represents the government. So what's so difficult about that?

The Indian has a little more difficulty in getting a drink. He can get a permit only on health grounds. Periodically he has to go to the Prohibition Medical Board and state his ailments—insomnia, loss of appetite, nervous tension, as the diagnosis of his family physician may be. The R.M.O. (Resident Medical Officer) takes his blood-pressure, a peon takes the weight, and in a few days the Indian applicant gets his Health Permit. Usually for two units. Of course most residents don't have time for all this. They cut out the red tape, just calling up their bootlegger. If they are honest with their government they just ask for two units, so that at least the spirit of the prohibition laws is maintained.

Social life in India, therefore, is much the same as life anywhere else, with the added attraction that you don't have to depend on a daily help to wash up the next day. It is also a misconception that Indian servants are treated like the old Roman slaves just because they don't get a TV set of their own. There is no TV to watch in the first place—and in any case my bearer much prefers his poker game, after serving dinner, in the garage below.

Oh yes, they play poker in India nowadays. What's more they play it well—as they do any game of bluff. You've got to get rid of the idea that most Indians are poor and have to walk, and the few who are rich ride elephants. Everyone in India is riding a high horse now. Mr Nehru started the fashion.

D. F. KARAKA

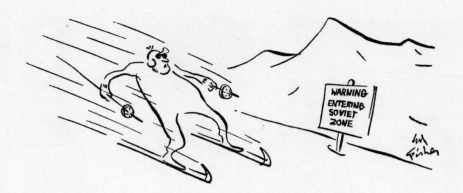

Epitaph for Harty

HERE'S the mortal part of Harty;
  In this life he got his start
Forming of a charter party
  Party of the second part.

Say not of him that he bartered,
  Chaffered crudely in the mart,
He who sat apart and chartered
  Parties with a loving heart.

To his parties he imparted
  Charters that were words of art,
Till the dreadful day he darted
  Underneath a dustman's cart.
Here he lies, the dear departed
  Party of the second part.

R. P. LISTER

135

'There you are! Fifty per cent nylon.'

WILLOWBROOK
EXPERIMENTAL FARM

thelwell

Sprod

'Feeling jaded? Spirits down?
Crumbly Hall for half a crown,
Open now for all to view—
Crumbly Hall the treat for you.'

PAW

cesc

Larry

'Take a letter to the Acme
Chair Company, Miss Fitzroy.'

'Eat up your plankton, dear, and
one of these days you'll grow up
to be an ash-tray.'

The Time of Being

IT gets hot in the cafe sometimes and then its really like hell working there. Not literally of course, though come to think of it I couldn't imagine much worse. Be a laugh if I had to spend eternity whiping down tables, I know our supervisor would be there for sure shaking her head at me for leaving a bit of potatoe while the fires licked up her legs. I'm thinking of going to purgatory though, its something a bit like a remand home.

Anyway one summer afternoon I saw this boy. You couldn't miss the way he came walking in with such a lordly air and sat down like he owned the place, at the same time withdrawing from his pocket a packet of lettuce sandwiches. I could tell they were lettuce because a bit dropped out on the floor where he hadn't pressed the bread together hard enough and there was a cabbage white butterfly catterpiller sitting on it. At least that proved it wasn't water cress though I suppose it might have been ordinary cress. I never really studied seriously the eating habbits of the cabbage white butterfly so I can't say if they only eat cabbage or not. From their name they do, but names are so misleading. Whoever heard of wigs for ears? My sister says you might twist their tails round like kiss curls, but if you did that somebody would be sure to report you for cruelty to insects. Honestly I do sometimes wonder if my sister is all there. I know its not very nice to say that but e.g. (for example), when I said I was writing this she told me with a frown. "Don't do that Mavis (my name is Mavis) it would be much easier if you sailed to the chanel islands on a raft and wrote a book called the 'Kontiki Expedition'." Then my brother who passed the eleven plus kind of sneered and said. "Don't be daft somebody already wrote a book called that." To which my sister replied, "So what? There must be hundred of people who haven't read it. Me for one." And that shows you how stupid she is because if I did write that book how would they know which was mine and which was the original? I shouldn't like to think I was taking money from anyones pocket same as I shouldn't like anyone to take money from mine.

Well the real reason I began to write was so that

people should have an idea of how we teenagers live. I mean nobody ever does write about us unless its something bad, and we should all know how the other half lives. Anyway this is a day in the life of a decent English rosebud.

It started when this fellow walked in the cafe and sat down with his duffel bag. I wasn't going to stand for that especially when he called me over casual like and asked me for a plate. So I put my hands on my hips and give him a smoldering look saying through parted lips. "There is a notice up there which says all food must have been brought on the premisis." And he bit into this egg calmly (I knew it was egg because after a bit you can tell can't you?) and said. "Well I did bring mine on the premisis or I wouldn't be eating it." I couldn't understand this very well. I mean I'm not dumb but when people start getting complicated I just expire. So I fetched him a plate and somehow or other we got to talking,

fashioned and I don't dig men messing about with my hair. I mean going to the hairdresser is a social occaison as much as anything and you can't talk to men about other women without they think you're being catty.

Its queer what can happen at the hairdressers. I must have had some of my most memorable experiances under the drier taken all round. I used to hide when mum took me there as a kid. They'd get frantic searching for me, but mum was always a bit disapointed when I turned up. And if they got me as far as the door I'd scream so that everyone ran off in the opposite direction, thinking I was being murdered.

She left me under the drier once. I smelt so strange when I came out. Did you ever smell burnt chips? And you should have seen my hair next morning. I didn't know if I should stay inside for six months, become a monk, or carry a sign saying

and before I knew where I was he had asked me to go out with him that night.

Now I had the afternoon off that day so I thought I'd get myself poshed up a bit. My friend you see she works in this hairdressers and she says I can always pop in for a hairdo when the're not busy. They don't get busy now so much. Some girls like a man breathing down their neck. But not me. I'm old

"Join The Yul Bryner Fan Club." Except that I daren't do that in case of the unions. So I had a cunning little crew cut.

This girl she does my hair real classy. Once she gave me one of these home perms. We didn't copy the chart though. I had some sausage curls at the back and a big wave on one side. Round my face she did some spit curls and it looked real smashing

when she finished. A fellow whistled sort of surprised when I came out, but I told him not to be cheeky and he didn't any more. Pity really.

I thought for this boy I would go special as I had never been with him before. Its best to break them in gently. So I had my hair given a gold rinse and swept off my face into a little bunch at the back which was tied with my expandable glitter ring. Then I pulled a bit forward and my friend cut it short and painted two or three lilac streaks in it like she read about in one of those magazines. It stuck out at the sides a bit but when I put on my pancake at home I stuck a gold sequin down low beside my mouth, and it looked so good that I stuck another beside my eye after I applied my purple eyeshadow.

Boy I was sexy. And this boy though so too because he recoiled. Recoiled, when he saw me. I did a little wriggle along the path and he laughed apreciatively as he watched me. He kept behind me down the street and I wriggled more than ever. I got a real good wriggle. My friend says I must have double jointed hips, but the way I do it actually is to tie my waspie belt just above my knees. Then I get my tight skirt on over the top. Its real murder but it gives you a smashing wriggle. And they don't tell you that in none of those beauty book for all they rush you half a doller.

Luckily the pictures are just round the corner and it didn't take us long to get there. Several people along the way seemed interested in the sky and did not reply to my jovial greeting. Perhaps they could see something though that I couldn't. They were friends of mine anyway. This boy I was with asked for two three shilling tickets and we were shown into the back row together.

As I remember it was a film about hospitals and they were just going to cut this woman open. Lovely it was, but as soon as the point of his scalper touched her skin they didn't show you any more. Just this mans face all gleaming and tense beneath the arc light. He kept muttering to himself all the while he was doing this operation, and I think it made this fellow beside me feel a bit queer because when I took his hand he clutched at me at first and then jumped away from me. "Oh I'm so sorry." I says. "I was thinking of my boy friend and I forgot he gave me up last week for another." And this boy gave me a sympathetic look from what I could see in the dimness, and we got on fine after that. I wonder what did happen to the boy I went with.

Well to get back to the thread of the story. When they showed us into the back row I imediatly thought "Hello!" Not because I had seen someone I knew but a figure of speech. "Hello!" I thought again as his arm stole round me. And casually with infinate care I removed my ivory handled toothpick from my bag and stuck it into the waistband of my skirt. I always carry it around with me for mum says you never know when you might need one.

We got settled down and then my friend Beatrix came along the row with a tray of refreshments round her neck. I called along the row in an attempt to discover what was the flavour of the month, and when she said it was strawberry which I don't like I asked if she had any left from last month. And the guy sitting next to me didn't like it a bit, not the one I came with but the one on the other side. Because I think he liked strawberry. He kept telling me to be quiet and I told him to be quiet too because I had been paid for. And after that he moved so I think he must have been a bit ashamed of himself.

The first film was not much good. But the second one was about this fellow with only a gitar to his name who made good. He was real gone and half way through this boy came up to me and bowing nicely ejaculated. "Come on, sugar, lets go and dig that crazy symphony." Oh and I couldn't refuse, he was so manley. Wow! Talk about posh. He had a longish coat on and ever such broad shoulders, and a real velvet collar. His trousers were tight, I mean tight. And cut off descretly at the bottom to show to advantage his green and black swede shoes with the three inch soles. He didn't wear one of them common string ties either but a cute little spotted bow. And when I stood up and he began to get hep I noticed that his shoes were cunningly low cut so as to give a tantilising glimpse of his luminous socks. They flashed out at me at intervals like the go sign on the traffic lights, and I was sent by them more than by his exquisite dancing. So much so that in a kind of trance I began to cry rythmically. "Go man go!" This insensed those of the comunity who had not yet risen and with animal cries they sprang to their feet. (I mean thats not my wording but what was in the paper the next morning). We clung 'till all exploded in a vivid red light and rocked absessed down the gangway.

Unfortunately after a bit we had to stop because I lost one of my sequins and had to get down on my hands and knees to look for it. Also I discovered on looking up that this fellows shoulder had gone.

Evidently in his mad stupor he had raised his arm too high in the process dislocating his shoulder pad. He hadn't lost it though. You could tell because he had a big lump sticking out of the middle of his back which wasn't there before. And when I told him he went off to do some running repairs.

Naturally after all this there was no stopping us and it was only when some little chap came running in yipping like a fiend that we paused amassed to watch. Occaisonally he pointed a starters pistol and with his eyes glinting with madness fixed on us he forced us back to the stalls. Isn't it astonishing what these older people will do to create an impression? He really made a spectecal of himself. This little fellow arrayed in imaculate black cutting off a strip down the front row of the one and nines and at intervals putting his hands over his ears while the fire burst from his pistol and a hail of blank caps piled up on the floor at his feet. And the while in the background the roar of music reached a pitch hitherto unrealized and soared into a resounding creshendo. Then suddenly the place became deadly quiet because the film had finished. And the only noise to be heard was the heavy breathing of the cats and an often unstiffled murmour from the usheretts crouching in the organ pit.

He turned to us his lips curling with the heat of the smoke rising from the gun in his hand. Then he barked "O.K. The shows finished." And with these memorable words he slowly walked backwards pushing his way through the swing doors of the organ pit. And climbing on the organ he rode alone to that fruitless waste where man has seldom been. Leaving us silent and awe struck. But then as The National Anthem began to play we recovered and moved as though by some pre-arranged signal in stately procession towards the exit.

HELENE DARREL

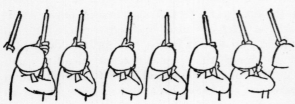

New Hat

My hat is like a hive for bees.
  My hat is like a mop.
It covers all my hair with ease.
  It's rather loose on top.

I must be careful of my face,
  Not raise my eyebrows, frown
Or move my ears about, in case
  My hat should slither down.

I stand before my looking-glass.
  I think how wonderful
That ever it should come to pass,
  This wig-like hulk of wool.

I *think* my fashion-sense can wring
  Grace from this shaggy dome.
I think I'd better hide the thing
  And quick. My husband's home.

ANDE

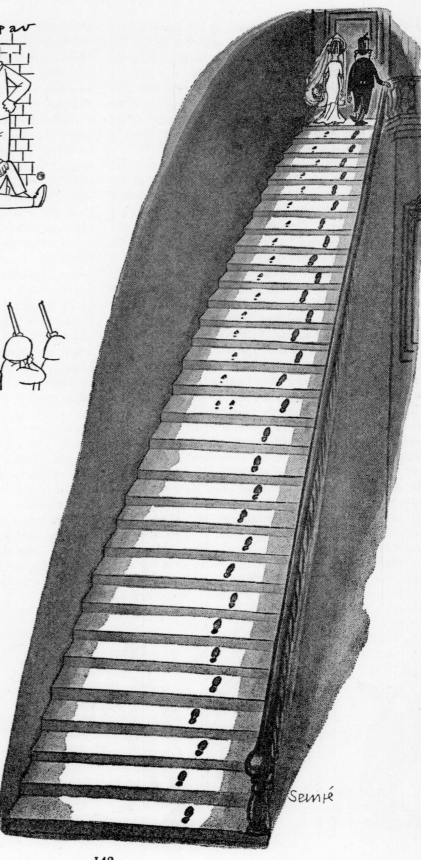

Shallow End

If Mr Chapman Pincher cares to announce that the seas around Britain are becoming steadily colder he will not lack a supporter. I am convinced, after a tour of the Devon littoral, that the English Channel has lost something like thirty degrees of temperature (Fahrenheit or Centigrade, call it what you will) during the past decade or so, and I cannot understand why the sea lanes from Torquay and other resorts are not already choked by pack or slob-ice.

On holiday I read with great interest about the polar voyage of the U.S. nuclear submarine *Nautilus*. A wonderful feat of navigation. But there was one point in Commander Anderson's report that made my lip curl involuntarily: "The temperature of the water under the ice cap was 32 degrees Fahrenheit (zero Centigrade)," he said, "and no trouble whatever was encountered". From this it seems fairly obvious that over the years there has been an exchange of waters between the North Pole and the English Channel. Commander Anderson wouldn't find Torbay so tepid, I can tell him . . .

I can tell him because I tried bathing in it. I stripped off on the sands (taking care, of course, that there were no chinks in the pyramid of deck-chairs constituting my modest refuge), paused only to execute a few setting-up exercises and smoke a couple of pipes, and then charged across the intervening slope of sand-with-flints.

As I crossed the threshold of pain to ankle depth some idiot boy of about six years threw a vulgar beach-ball in my direction. The thing hit the water perhaps four yards from me and the resultant fine spray of icicles made me shut my eyes very tight. Beach balls are the devil's own invention and should not be allowed between high and low water by any resort interested in retaining the custom of men in my age-group.

I was now twenty yards and about two feet of slush and infrigerated seaweed from the children. They yelled for me to join them, but I was far too busy watching the wavelets and timing my frenetic tip-toe attempts to avoid further immersion to make any friendly reply. Years ago the really shallow water in the Channel was lukewarm, like a wartime Algerian wine; now it is a fishmonger's slab under the hose. But I was not going to be licked by a few inches of agony. I stooped, cupped some of the stuff in my hands and tentatively applied it to my shins and thighs. And suddenly the wind became merci-lessly frigid. I looked back to the deck-chairs hoping to see a man hawking afternoon papers and lunch-time cricket scores. I saw nothing but a blur of grinning faces. Had I been able I should have blushed.

Ten yards to my right four stoutish women were standing waist-deep amid the alien ice. They looked reasonably serene and it occurred to me with unreasonable pleasure that the cruel sea sometimes contains pockets of warmer water. These ladies, I reasoned, might have found such a pocket. I moved towards them.

"Come on dad," said one of them, "we won't bite you."

"It's all right once you've got your hair wet," said another.

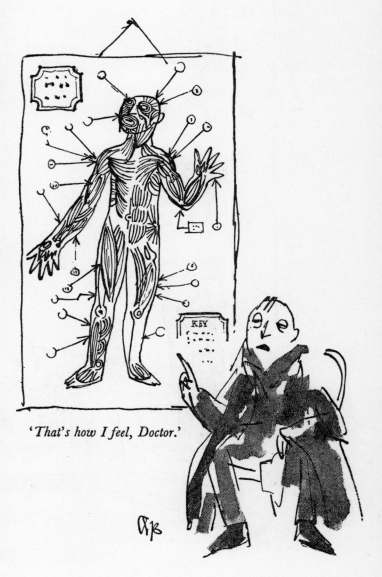

'*That's how I feel, Doctor.*'

"If you've got any to get wet," laughed the one in tasteless yellow sateen.

"Have a heart," said four, "the men feels it worse'n we do—they got their bones nearer the surface."

"Count three, ducks," said the yellow bladder, "and take the plunge. Won't kill you."

"It's much warmer in than out," said the one in green-and-blue candy stripes.

My jaws and teeth were vibrating like the bonnet of an old bus, so I made no attempt to counter this badinage. Instead, I tried a smile. I put my less lifeless foot forward, encountered some treacherous depression in the ocean bed and immediately took the full impact of the Channel round my hips. And now I knew the meaning of fear. How long was it since lunch? It could be fatal, I remembered, to bathe on a full stomach. Wasn't it Napoleon or somebody who said as much about his army? And that extra king-size pain behind the left knee. Cramp? I hoped so.

I found myself on dry sand. The children were watching from what seemed the shelter of the French coast. "Too shallow," I shouted, the wind whistling my words away at right angles, "I'm going round to the jetty to get a real dive into the harbour. Don't be late for tea." And I ran—after the manner of Herb Elliott—until I was lost to their view and the cackling of the four insensitive ladies among the crowd milling round the comic post-cards, toffee-apples and candy floss.

I read the lunch-time scores in the delicious warmth of the Hall of Mirrors. There was another long article about Commander Anderson and the *Nautilus*. I read that too.

BERNARD HOLLOWOOD

'*Anything to avoid tackling people face to face, that's you, isn't it?*'

144

Roy Davis

TORSO

Spring Begins at Fifty

At about this time of year there comes, I suppose, to almost every man and woman a strong desire to be elsewhere. The long dark days and the lack of sunlight have taken their toll; so have the long articles by newspaper doctors pointing out what a toll the long dark days have taken. Mind and body cry out for a change, for re-creation as the vicar so cleverly puts it. Pictures form in the mind of the place where one would like to be.

My own wants are simple. I require to be leaning over an old stone bridge, within a hundred yards of a white-fronted inn and half an hour of lunch. There must be rising ground somewhere about, with trees in their first leaf and the water that flows beneath the bridge must be shallow, somewhat broken, and free from old hip-baths. The only noise should be bird-song, and not too much of that, the only smell a hint of wood-smoke. The sun shines warmly down on this pleasant picture and after a while, when I have

exahusted the immediate delights of running water, an old man comes along and says good-day. There was a time, I dare say, when a young woman would have entered into this springtime dream-sequence, but not now. If fifty young women walked across the bridge, equipped to launch between them a full fifty thousand ships, I should not bother to turn my head, well knowing that they would not in any case bother to turn theirs. What I want now is an old, old man, so old that one look at him makes me feel by comparison almost springy, lissome as a sapling, capable if the mood took me of laying one hand on the parapet and vaulting lightly over into the glancing waters. I want him to dodder and totter as he comes along; yet there must be an aged brightness, a geniality about him, so that he is ready enough to pass the time of day with a stranger and not too dim and rheumy of eye to note the breadth of chest beneath the new Harris tweed jacket, the lounging grace of the scarcely shrunken limbs, the relaxed strength of a face enriched rather than dishevelled by the etchings of middle-age.

If this does not seem a very amiable or noble wish, this desire for a decrepit foil to heighten my sense of euphoria, it has to be remembered that the long dark days have taken their toll. It is every man for himself in the spring. Nor, in fact, am I doing this old, old man any harm by imagining his presence on the bridge. He will not grudge me the lighter burden of my years, nor be tempted to take a cut with his stick at the less arthritic of my two shapely knees. On the contrary he will be courteous and friendly, as age is to youth, and any envy he may show will certainly be feigned. That is the law of life. If some young stripling of twenty comes striding over the bridge *I* shall not envy his elastic gait nor grudge the ease with which he carries a folding tent, three blankets, shirts, socks, spirit lamp and other accessories on his back. I shall fall naturally into my more senile role, prepared, if the young man pauses long enough to confide his hopes of being over the Black Mountains before sundown, to adopt an "Ah-me . . . *O-mihi-præteritos . . . Et-ego-in-Arcadia*" attitude which will send him on his way with redoubled satisfaction in his own youth and vigour. But it is nonsense to suggest that I shall be in any way depressed or soured by his ability to be over the mountains by sundown. The sooner the better as far as I am concerned. What matters to me is that I shall be in the white-fronted inn by one o'clock with ease—which is more than this poor old dodderer now approaching me over the bridge could manage. And *he* doesn't care about *my* glowing health and newly-pressed drill trousers. Why should he? He is on his way to patronize some even older crony who can no longer get out at all on a fine spring morning.

Dear me, these vernal longings are leading me into strange, un-Christian channels. But it is nice to be honest once in a while. At least I no longer desire, as men in their thirties do when April approaches, to beat all my neighbours at tennis or make a hundred runs at some poor bowler's expense. I only want to lean against this old stone parapet, delighting in the play of the sunshine on the cuffs of my new drip-dry shirt (with spare collar, 63*s.*), and bask in the conviction that I am not yet nearly as old and desiccated as I was in January. It does not seem much to ask.

Even so, it is too much. I see now, on re-reading what I have written, that I have allowed myself a new Harris tweed jacket, drill trousers with creases, *and* a three-guinea shirt. Imagination has outrun discretion. It is not the expense I am thinking of,

though there is that, but the impropriety. Youthful as I know I shall feel when this yearning to be elsewhere comes to fruition, it will still not suit me to dress like an undergraduate who has come into money. At that rate I shall be wearing buckskin shoes and a college blazer in my sixties and start rounding up adolescents for a game of table tennis. This strong equinoctial craving for new clothes to match the rejuvenation of the spirit has to be kept in check. Give me a country suit with that gentlemanly run-in look, a shooting-stick, and a small moustache to match the touch of grey at my temples and let me watch the darting sand-martins with the level, faintly amused gaze of one who looks back without regret to his salad days, and forward with undimmed eagerness to lunch.

The picture is now complete. The river lisps and mutters pleasantly against the piers. The stone is warm to the touch. Everywhere the sap is rising, and in my deep heart's core there is a feeling that nothing, no feat of endurance or athletic prowess, is beyond me. Only I no longer care, if I may put it so without immodesty, to show off.

H. F. ELLIS

'The oil pollution here must be simply dreadful.'

Hypnotic Fit

ALTHOUGH my waist is badly placed and not so very slender,
Although my hips have strained their zips and snapped a back suspender,
Although my feet are far from neat, my calves are second-grade,
In spite of this I never miss a Mannequin Parade.
I love to gape at style and shape in growing sweet confusion
Till they have twined about my mind a one-with-them illusion,
And I may buy what takes my eye, convinced that I can wear it;
For those with hips to strain their zips have lips to grin and bear it.

HAZEL TOWNSON

149

Keep Them In, Alderman Says

CHRISTOPHER HOLLIS *discusses a new aspect of the racial troubles*

THE serious class riots in which Etonians have been recently involved at the railway stations of Datchet and Wraysbury must cause all responsible citizens to ask themselves whether this nation can any longer afford to allow totally unregulated migration of Etonians to and fro across the country.

The last thing that we wish to do is to suggest that an Etonian is in himself worse than any other school-boy. It is by no fault of his that he is an Etonian. Any suggestion of inferiority would be an illiberal suggestion, smacking of prejudice. Nor is it the individual Etonian who creates the problem. The problem is the problem of numbers. It only becomes acute when Etonians insist, as unfortunately they do, on herding together in one particular area. They live there in houses, many of which are old and insanitary and some of which contain thirty or as many as forty boys each, in conditions of gross overcrowding, such as would not be tolerated in any housing estate that was subject to public control. Their numbers are growing fast. We do not say that their way of life is inferior to that of the ordinary Englishman. To make such a suggestion would be narrow-minded, but it is —we must face it—different. The Etonian has not got the ordinary Englishman's liking for quiet. The citizen of Eton or of Windsor likes on a summer evening to stroll tranquilly along the river's side or to take his ease upon the water. Is it altogether surprising that he should complain if he finds the towing path jammed with a shouting mass of excited schoolboys, encouraging with frantic cries their fellows who are rowing against one another in some race? Can he be blamed if he finds such excitement not altogether English? One has only to walk through the streets of Eton at night and it is possible to hear through the open windows a noise that is sometimes almost deafening of shouting and raucous laughter. There are those among the so-called scholars who occupy themselves by playing in a jazz band, while —even worse—among the larger boys are to be found, sometimes, pockets of Greek-speaking and Latin-speaking pupils who seem to make little effort to assimilate themselves to the general customs of the land in which they live.

It is of course true that in a civilized society persons of widely different social origins must learn to live amicably together. There is need for tolerance on both sides and we are well aware that each has much to learn from the other. We have nothing but praise for the admirable enterprise of those public-spirited citizens who have attempted to make friends of the Etonian, to invite him into their houses and to try to integrate him into the British way of life. But in spite of all such efforts there remains the great intractable problem—the problem of intermarriage. As a general rule of course the Etonian will always prefer to marry the sister of a fellow Etonian. Beyond question the repugnance of the Etonian to the notion of intermarriage is in general every bit as strong as the repugnance of the non-Etonian. But it is idle to shut our eyes to it that, if totally free social intercourse between Etonian and non-Etonian is permitted, mixed marriages will inevitably from time to time occur. Is society prepared for that? It is not sufficient to dismiss the problem with sonorous generalities. Each one of us must face it as a real and personal problem and ask himself: Would you be prepared for your sister to marry an Etonian?

As Mr Justice Pumpkin so truly said, every boy has a right to walk freely about the streets of this land, whatever the colour of his tie, and it is indeed far best that this difficult problem should be settled by agreement between the Government and the authorities of the school rather than by unilateral administrative action. There is, happily, good reason to think that such a solution may be found. We would not ask that the Government should close down the school, but it cannot be to the interest of the school any more than it is to that of society at large that its numbers be wholly unregulated. No news could be more welcome than the news that the headmaster had of his own volition decided to expel some four or five hundred of the boys, thus reducing the problem of flogging the rest to one of manageable proportions. Such a measure, if taken by the school authorities themselves, could not fairly be represented as a measure of discrimination. The open-barred prison may have its contribution to make to the solution of the problems of penal reform, but no one is a worse friend to such reforms than he who advocates its too rapid or too indiscriminate adoption.

'Mrs Hinkley!'

Pacific Intentions

"You don't have to go to Tahiti to find straw huts beside a warm blue sea, to explore deserted sun-drenched islands, to wear a sarong and dance barefoot under the stars—at the Club's holiday villages in the MEDITERRANEAN you can enjoy the South Seas way of life for only £40!"

Advertisement in THE TIMES

WHEN you're sick of your civilization,
  When you're feeling restrained and repressed,
When you long to be noisy and nerveless,
  To be decadent, drunk and undressed,
You don't have to go to Tahiti
  To wear your sarong with a swing:
We can find you instead a place in the Med.
  Which is just like the genuine thing.

You don't have to go to Tahiti
  To exorcize civilized man,
But make for the Mediterranean,
  Where civilization began.
You don't have to seek the Pacific
  To find atavistic release:
Provided your mind is sufficiently blind,
  You can manage it cheaper in Greece.

B. B.-P. DURHAM

'Not yet, you damn fool.'

151

Exceptional People

Things you've seen, people you've met, What about a book, what? I mean.

"SOME streak of diffidence, perhaps. Dub it rank laziness if you will."

"I dub it rank laziness."

"Albeit *l'affaire* de Brett has more than once tempted me to essay authorship."

"To which de Brett do you refer?"

"To Ada de Brett; she of the multi-millions and the many enemies, inevitable concomitants of a ruthless and beautiful woman's climb to the peak. She filled her house with delinquent parasites, brushing aside the frightened protests of her uncle Jim, a v.c. of the old school who had watched over Ada since Eastbourne."

"Then Jim murdered her for her money?"

"Gradually (she was twenty-five at the time, and apparently in good health) she became afflicted with cramps, difficulty in walking, and other symptoms of peripheral neuritis. Naturally we all concluded she was the victim of slow arsenic poisoning of which

also these are symptoms. We'd called in the Yard, alerted the Coroner and forced Jim to return his v.c. to the War Office when the amazing truth leaked out. She had peripheral neuritis. How we all laughed."

"What a figure of a woman! I'd like to meet someone like her."

"*Non possumus*, old boy. Forty-five years later she was found brutally battered to death in the shrubbery."

"Uncle had struck at last."

"Thirty people could, and gladly would, have done it, but it was finally proved to be the work of a passing tramp."

"Jove, Maitland, you whet my appetite for the strange, not to say unusual."

"Avid for copy, to employ the jargon of Fleet Street, eh? De Brutt was an interesting fellow, too."

"You knew him? This beats cock-fighting! Who was he?"

"Thief, near-matricide (and would have been so

'*Look, dear, let me 'phone the garage.*'

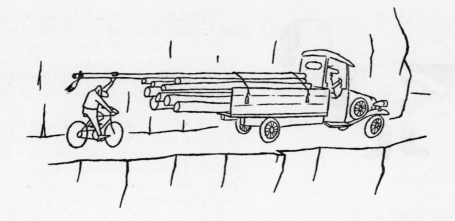

wholly had not dry-rot weakened the broken chair-leg he used as a weapon in that wretched shabby-genteel villa in the Harrow Road which was their home), and one to whom women were but playthings, or stepping stones."

"Where was he stepping to?"

"Fame, and riches beyond the dreams of avarice. He had made up his mind to be the greatest film and TV star ever known, and little did he reck what lives were wrecked as he strode to his goal."

"But surely some girl, who knew the beast behind the mask, watched and waited, determined to expose him at the very pinnacle of his success?"

"Certainly she did. Name of Myra. She's still waiting. After riding roughshod over all that decent men deemed sacred, he turned out to be a total flop. Couldn't even get a booking for a matinée turn on the pier."

"But surely his agent, versed in mass psychology and the dubious skills of modern publicity, built up an image of this untalented scallywag as a top-line genius and hero-figure for millions who little guessed?"

"That's all de Brutt asked him to do, but the agent said he hadn't the time. De Brutt had to go back and apologize to his mother and Myra."

"And they forgave?"

"How could they? They'd assumed he'd win international acclaim, and then they'd sell the dirt on him to the Sunday newspapers. The question then was: What would de Brutt do next?"

"Enthralling indeed."

"Very. I've often wondered myself. But I lost touch with him about then. Naturally from time to time a rumour is whispered in the Harrow Road. They said de Brutt was behind the great greyhound-doping conspiracy which set the public agog a few years ago."

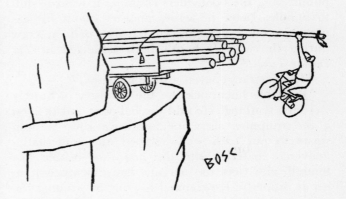

"And it was he?"

"Of course not. Don't you read the papers? That was three other fellows. No connection with de Brutt at all."

"What a career. You should write it, man, write it, write it."

"I would if I could remember that agent's initials. Don't want to leave a gap in the story."

"Ah! You meticulous old stickler! Not for you the turmoil of modern journalism. Rather than leave a fact unchecked you'd let the mighty rotary presses turn in vain. Yet in that capacious head of yours what secrets are stored—of the great, the near great, and . . . the notorious. I rejoice to find you in reminiscent vein."

"Well, I used to have the privilege of an occasional chat with de Bratt."

"You mean *the* de Bratt?"

"No, no. The other. The one who played for England for forty-two years and wrote *Inside the M.C.C.*"

"The book that caused so little sensation some time ago? Where he said they were all very good fellows without any special idiosyncrasies or quirks of temperament?"

ROY DAVIS

"It was withdrawn from the bookshops soon after publication, the booksellers claiming it was too dull to handle. Later he wrote another about his experiences on a little-known barrage balloon crew during the war. It hasn't been serialized in *The Sunday Times*."

"That's strange, even a little uncanny."

"Probably his attacks on the Ministry of Supply were too scathing. He said the balloons and the rest of the equipment were fine, and it was sheer wanton waste to put such well-designed and punctually-delivered material into the hands of people like himself who were too nervous and incompetent to use it properly. He claimed his role in winning the war was negligible compared to that played by the General Staffs of Britain and her Allies."

"Some people will do anything for a little cheap publicity. Fancy him daring to impugn a man like him. Why, he's not fit to lick his own boots."

"Deep down inside he knows that. He says it's lumbago. But he carries on. None of the big newspapers has published the story of his time in Paris with John Foster Dulles and Sophia Loren."

"The trio met?"

"Naturally they didn't meet. Why on earth should they? After all, Dulles happens to be the American Secretary of State, and Miss Loren is a famous film star, whereas de Bratt was just one more down-at-heel British tourist. He makes the whole thing perfectly clear in his article."

"Certainly a bizarre experience."

"Not more so than that of de Britt. Jever give a passing thought to road accidents?"

"Yes—and no."

"De Britt found out about them. It's the wheel."

"Of Fate?"

"No metaphorician, de Britt. When he said wheel he meant wheel, and be damned to your whole pack of long-haired figures of speech. He attacked the wheel as such."

"Great heavens, Maitland, surely that was carrying iconoclasm beyond all reasonable bounds! One needs but consult the nearest book of reference, or reputable thinker, to learn that the discovery of the wheel, almost on a par with the discovery of fire, marked one of the great epochs in the advance of humanity."

"That was the story that was put about. De Britt, grudging himself aught but a crust of bread while he pursued his researches, reached the conclusion that the claims made for the wheel were fraudulent. There was a basic flaw, he proved, in the whole conception of the wheel. The idea of the wheel, as such, does not, he found, bear scientific scrutiny."

"It had been foisted?"

"On an all too gullible public. De Britt devoted his remaining energies and his meagre savings to the task of exposing the wheel."

"But the great wheel interests, I make no doubt, thwarted him at every turn. Their ramifications, I dare avow, are world-wide, their tentacles everywhere—aye, even in the very heart of the Body Politic."

"Yet undaunted, filled with burning faith that truth must prevail, de Britt laid the facts before the Ministry of Labour."

"And their self-styled experts, one surmises, laughed, yes positively laughed him to scorn. Was the dead hand of tradition alone responsible for their essentially Bourbon attitude? Or was some still more sinister and—no, I *will* speak out—corrupting influence at work?"

"Neither. The officials, with the country's good at heart, listened attentively, introduced him to the Minister and took him to tea at No. 10 Downing Street where he was received with every mark of courtesy and respect. He was given an *ex gratia* payment of £1,000,000 and appointed Perpetual Adviser to the Ministry for fear that genius might still go unrecognized—de Britt is an insignificant looking runt—photographs of him were circulated to police stations above the caption 'This is de Britt the Genius. Be sure to recognize him if you see him.' The wheel is on the way out."

"You know, my trained journalistic instinct tells me there may be a story in this. It's got wheel-appeal. Believe I'll give this de Britt a buzz."

"Do, my dear fellow, by all means. I count myself fortunate if an idle fellow's chatter has brought some grist to your mill. Personally I have more grist than I can use. Call me on the blower any time you want some."

CLAUD COCKBURN

Babylonians in My Life

WHEN I was at school, except for Boadicea, Alfred's cakes and Harold's eyeful of arrow, there just wasn't any history before 1485. Before that it was all flint-axes, protoplasm and Sir Mortimer Wheeler.

Nowadays, as my daughter has taught me, the school-teachers start right at the beginning. My daughter is nine, hula-hooped and nautical, and has a thing about Nelson. On our last visit to London we went to Greenwich to see the grisly holes in his tunic and underwear, and noted that the log of the *Victory* was in the British Museum.

So next day to Bloomsbury, and we located the log in the Manuscript Room.

"He was very brave," she said, leaning over the case. "But he wasn't a very good writer. I don't think Miss Chater would have given him any stars."

"The sea was stormy," I said, "and he only had one arm. I'd like to see your Miss Chater produce any copper-plate in a rough sea with one arm tied behind her back."

"It must be hard to write with one arm. How do you hold the paper straight?"

"You could hold it with your stump."

"Supposing you hadn't got a stump?"

"Well—I suppose you could lean down and hold it with your chin."

"Then you'd probably stick yourself in the face with your pen-nib. How would *you* write if somebody cut your arm off? Right up to here."

"I'd use a typewriter."

"But how would you hold down the key for capitals?"

"With a pencil in my teeth."

"But supposing they took out all your teeth, as well?"

I hadn't come all the way to the British Museum for one of her crazy inquisitions. I can get them at breakfast any day just by lowering the paper to find my nerve-tonic. To distract her from the one-armed problem I said "Come and see an Egyptian mummy".

It worked and we went upstairs. I never realized before just how many mummies we taxpayers have got stored away in those long, quiet acres of Egyptian Rooms in Bloomsbury. Rows and rows of them, two and three in a bed, and standing-room only for junior members.

She enjoyed herself reading the recipe for mummy-

'How many purposes should one have?'

155

making, especially the part about scooping out the brains and viscera and putting them into canopic jars, and then we wandered out of the mummy section and into the heart of Egyptology. Before us, as far as the eye could see, stretched a vista of glass-filled, clay-coloured rooms. We were the only moving objects in a silent petrified aquarium, and the peace—brother, it was wonderful!

Before you throw up the whole thing, shave your head and go into that monastery, try a few Friday afternoons in the Third Egyptian Room. Knots untied inside my head and inner tensions flowed out of my ears as we drifted among the eternal silences of tablets, urns, scarabs and amulets, everything rain-washed, desiccated, age-old and broken. I was drinking in the tranquillity and studying a nineteenth dynasty lipstick holder when my daughter put paid to peace and holy quiet.

"There it is!" she yelled, pointing into the distance. "That's it! Just like the picture in Miss Chater's history book!"

And off she went at full gallop, whooping in excitement, dragging me one-handed behind her. Our shoes clattered like sacrilege on the parquet, her shouts and my complaints echoed through the marble halls, hidden professors bobbed up from behind statues, attendants appeared from nowhere. . . . On we went, like the hammers of hell, belting back through the dynasties, a thousand years passing at every stride, weaving among cat-gods, side-stepping sacred crocodiles, swerving round cases of cuneiform.

"What is it?" I gasped. "What's sent you off your head?"

"Hammurabi!" she yelled. "There it is, Hammurabi and the Sun-god."

Two of the professors joined in and ran along beside us. One was just curious, the other thought the place was on fire.

"Don't panic," he muttered as he loped along. "For God's sake, don't panic."

Electric bells like burglar-alarms started to ring all over the building . . . where once peace had reigned was now all pandemonium . . . an attendant came suddenly into our path . . . if he hadn't ducked behind a Coptic bull we'd have trampled him to death. . . . Back through the Assyrians we raced—a hundred kings flashed by . . . great empires died in the wind of our passing . . . a few more millenniums saw the shape of our heels and we were clear through to the Babylonian Room.

"There it is," she said, shooting diagonally across to the left-hand corner and shrieking to a stop before a large dark monolith about eight feet high. "Isn't it wonderful? Fancy me finding the Hammurabi Stone all by myself!"

Her eyes were beacons of delight, she held out a tender hand and caressed the girt block of basalt. To her it was clearly the end of the rainbow, the most wonderful surprise of her life. To me it was just big, black and scratched.

"That's the Sun-god," she said, pointing to the picture carved on the top quarter. "And he's giving the laws to Hammurabi."

"Who's Hammurabi?" I asked.

The curious professor came up.

"My dear man," he said, looking at me as if I'd appeared in his apple, "don't you know who Hammurabi was?"

"No," I said. "I'm sorry."

"I know," said my daughter, "he was King of Babylon and he made the first laws."

"That's right," said the professor. "And this is the Hammurabi Stone. Now, down here, it tells you all about it . . . "

My daughter and the professor knelt down on the floor and discussed the scratches. The attendant came over and joined in. I turned to speak to the professor who thought we were on fire, but he avoided me and knelt down with the rest. They hate you if you're uneducated.

I tried once or twice to get into the conversation, but they froze me out. I wandered over to the other side of the room where a man was polishing the floor around a fragment of Ur.

"Good afternoon," I said. "Not many draws up last week, were there?"

"No," he said. "But I got six up though. Arsenal did me a bad turn."

"Did they?" I said. "They've been a bit chancey all the season."

"You can't trust 'em no more. They ain't like the old days, are they?"

"No," I said. "They ain't."

We got on to talking about the virtues of the block four-by-four perm over the any four pairs from eight, and I bet those Hammurabi experts wouldn't have understood a blind word we were saying. They clammed up after about ten minutes, shook hands all round and my daughter came to collect me.

"Miss Chater is going to go right through the ceiling with surprise," she said, "when I tell her I've actually seen the Hammurabi Stone. She may have a picture of it in her history book but I bet she's never been all the way to the British Museum to see it."

Down in the hall we asked the post-card counter for a picture of the Stone.

"I'm sorry," said the young woman, "but we do not keep any postcards of the Hammurabi Stone. There is not sufficient demand."

My daughter was thunderstruck. It was all I could do to get her out of the place without setting about somebody. Going down the steps she carried on just like a grown woman.

"Fancy that! Did you ever hear anything like it? No postcards of the Hammurabi Stone. *Everybody* knows about the Hammurabi Stone. It's the very first picture in the history book. You'd think they'd have a postcard of anything important like that."

At the gates she turned and sneered back at the building.

"Well, I don't think much of that museum, I must say. Not a patch on that one at York. They had picture postcards of simply everything there. . . ."

The British Museum shrank back a pace into the evening shadows and we left it to its shame.

PATRICK RYAN

INDEX OF AUTHORS AND ARTISTS

INDEX OF AUTHORS AND ARTISTS